SHOWgrins

SHOWgrins

Women Who Walk on Water

The Third Book in Award-Winning Author Betty Collier's
Living Inside The Testimony® Book Series

Betty Collier

Website: showgrins.com
Website: livinginsidethetestimony.com

Special thanks to Paula Sosin for her priceless contribution to the book cover design. Paula is a Sjögren's patient and also a graphic designer. You can read her story beginning at Chapter 19.

Library of Congress Control Number:		2013900916
ISBN:	Hardcover	978-1-4797-8016-7
	Softcover	978-1-4797-8015-0
	Ebook	978-1-4797-8017-4

This book was printed in the United States of America.

To order additional copies of this book, contact:
Xlibris Corporation
1-888-795-4274
www.Xlibris.com
Orders@Xlibris.com
123805

CONTENTS

Celebrity Panel

I would like to express heartfelt gratitude to Steven Taylor, chief executive officer of the Sjögren's Syndrome Foundation, the only national nonprofit organization focused on increasing research, education, and awareness for Sjögren's syndrome. Thank you for guiding me in the right direction and introducing me to these five remarkable women. I am excited about our partnership and look forward to contributing half of the proceeds from this book to the Sjögren's Syndrome Foundation.

My sincerest appreciation and admiration is extended to the five fabulous book contributors who are known as my celebrity panel: Cathy Taylor, Estrella Bibbey, Judy Kang, Lynn Petruzzi, and Paula Beth Sosin. Thank you for opening your hearts to me and sharing your Sjögren's stories with the world. By disclosing so much of yourselves and revealing the intimate details of your journeys, you have inspired, encouraged, and motivated many others facing crossroads in their lives.

Venus Williams, thank you for everything. If it wasn't for you, I never would have written this book!

Increasing Awareness Begins Today

Chapter 1

Fame, Fortune, and Fatigue

WHO WOULDN'T WANT to be like Venus Williams, one of the most admired professional athletes in the world? Continue reading for about three or four minutes, and I'll answer that question. But, first, let's take a quick glance at the trophy room of this phenomenal tennis superstar. She has won an astonishing forty-three singles titles, including two U.S. Open Singles and five Wimbledon Singles. Along with her sister Serena Williams, she has also won an amazing nineteen doubles titles, which include two at the U.S. Open Doubles, two at the French Open Doubles, five at the Wimbledon Doubles, and four at the Australian Open Doubles. And, lastly, she has been an Olympic gold medal tennis champion for an unprecedented four times.

In addition to her tennis accolades, Williams is CEO of her interior design firm, V Starr Interiors, and realized a dream come true by launching her fashion line, EleVen. She has been recognized by Forbes on numerous occasions such as Forbes's *World's 100 Most Powerful Women*. *Most Powerful Black Women in the U.S.*, and *Celebrity 100*. If that's not enough, she's also part-owner of the Miami Dolphins along with her sister Serena, making them the first African-American females with ownership in an NFL franchise.

So why am I talking about Williams in my book? After all, she wrote a New York Times best seller, a book entitled *Come to Win: Business Leaders, Artists, Doctors, and Other Visionaries on How Sports Can Help You Top Your Profession*. What does her book have to do with my book? *Absolutely nothing*. However, this book does have a lot to do with Williams. You see, Williams had to pull out of the U.S. Open in 2011 due to yet another undertaking, undoubtedly her toughest challenge yet, one that up to four million Americans are also battling to live with.

Williams is fighting Sjögren's syndrome, the second most common autoimmune disease. Prior to her announcement, Sjögren's syndrome was probably the most common, unknown disease in the world, even though it was first identified in 1933 by Dr. Henrik Sjögren.

Classic symptoms are dry eyes and dry mouth, but Sjögren's may also cause dysfunction of organs such as the kidneys, gastrointestinal system, blood vessels, lungs, liver, pancreas, and the central nervous system. Williams, along with millions of others, experience extreme fatigue and joint pain, which is likely why she had to withdraw from the tournament.

I will ask the question again. Who wouldn't want to be like Venus Williams? Up to four million Americans can answer in the affirmative, with approximately 3,600,000 of them being females. I think I am one of them. I have not been formally diagnosed yet, but I am seeing the specialist my primary care physician referred me to. Before I finish writing this book, I will know for sure if I have it, but that's another chapter toward the end of the book.

For now, let's see what happened after Williams pulled out of the U.S. Open. I read a story on the internet a couple of days after she withdrew, *Venus Williams Battles Sjögren's Syndrome*. Needless to say, my curiosity got the best of me. I wondered how she could have such a dreadful disease that forced her to leave the tournament after only one match. Would she ever be able to return to this sport that she loved and once ruled?

Much to my surprise, the article only had two paragraphs about Williams. She was quoted as saying, "I am thankful I finally have a diagnosis and am now focused on getting better and returning to the court soon." The rest of the article was about the disease, not Williams. It was only one day after reading Williams had to withdraw that I began writing the first chapter of this book.

As I was trying to comprehend what had happened to me over those twenty-four hours, I had already self-diagnosed myself as being affirmed with this same condition, and I was now totally obsessed with writing a book about it to help others. I just wish Dr. Smith had identified the illness instead of Dr. Sjögren. Hence the book title, *SHOWgrins*, because I read that Sjögren's is pronounced "SHOW-grins." In my haste to start writing this book the very next day, I entitled it *SHOWgrins,* so I wouldn't forget how to pronounce my new diagnosis and new book title.

So how does this story fit into my book series of uplifting, real-life, inspirational testimonies? Let's see what Venus Williams had to say about all of this.

Chapter 2

What Did Venus Have to Say About All of This?

"I'M REALLY DISAPPOINTED to have to withdraw from this year's U.S. Open," Williams said in a 2011 statement. She went on to say, "I have recently been diagnosed with Sjögren's syndrome, an autoimmune disease which is an ongoing medical condition that affects my energy level and causes fatigue and joint pain."

Venus had thoroughly enjoyed playing her first match and truly wanted to continue playing, but she was unable to do so. Her body was being attacked by itself, which seems to be cruel and unusual punishment considering the extreme amount of time she has labored and conditioned her body to be in top-notch "tennis shape." Being afflicted by one of the most prevalent yet misunderstood autoimmune disorders that exists today could have meant the end of her spectacular tennis career.

But wait a minute. We're talking about Venus Williams, the world class athlete who has won ten tournaments in the last four years despite feeling fatigued and having difficulty breathing, symptoms that can now be attributed to Sjögren's.

"The fatigue is hard to explain unless you have it," Williams said. "Some mornings, I feel really sick, like when you don't get a lot of sleep or you have a flu or cold. I always have some level of tiredness. And the more I tried to push through it, the tougher it got."

Williams said she had struggled with fatigue for years but never knew the cause of it until her recent diagnosis. People who suffer from Sjögren's can appear to be perfectly healthy, even though they do not have the energy level to raise their arms sometimes. Like other patients with Sjögren's, Williams said the disease made her feel tired, which is a gross understatement to say the least.

It is often impossible to alleviate that fatigue sensation. Even when exercising, these patients use much more oxygen than healthy people, although no one knows why.

Prior to finally being diagnosed, Williams said, "I'd go to doctors, but I never got any answers, so there was nothing I could do but keep going. It was frustrating, always being in the dark and not having anything to help me but my own will." Because Sjögren's causes so many symptoms, oftentimes, it's hard even for a specialist to get a full understanding and see the big picture. Patients like Williams look much better than they feel and may go years before being treated for this disease that is so routinely undiagnosed and untreated.

Often labeled as hypochondriacs, depressed, psychotic, emotional, attention seekers, or menopausal, patients sometimes accept the labels and never receive the medical care they so desperately need to improve their quality of life. Some even tend to ignore the symptoms until they become debilitating. When Williams was diagnosed, she said, "You almost get used to having all these symptoms. You tell yourself to shake it off. Just keep going. Over time, you do start to wonder what's happening and if you're going crazy."

What a relief it was for her to finally have an explanation and justification for the way she was feeling all those years. She had definitely fit the mold of a Sjögren's patient. She looked a lot better than she felt.

Venus's sister Serena Williams said in a statement, "I think she's really happy now that she knows what it is after all this time. I think, if anything, it's going to help her now to treat it and go forward." Serena believes Venus's life has changed for the better now that she has been diagnosed.

Throughout her career, Venus has routinely refused to discuss injuries and illnesses. She adapted the attitude that if she was in a tournament, then she was healthy enough to play. But with this energy-sapping disease, Venus said, "A lot of the battle is just trying to be fit and stay healthy. Sometimes, I've been losing that battle a lot."

"My biggest challenge now is learning how to live like this," Venus said. "I don't know how I am going to be." Sometimes she can hardly even get out of bed because her joints hurt so terribly bad. "I'm no longer in control of my life. That's what it's like for me now. I suppose though it could be a lot worse," she said.

When Venus reflects back on her career, she realizes that Sjögren's has silently affected it in a monumental way. "I've been playing a lot of matches with a half a deck," she said. "I have to be up for every match because people come out against me with nothing to lose." So how can she play with a tennis racket that sometimes feels like concrete in her hand?

Williams said, "A lot of times, I've had to pretend I felt good when I felt terrible." She remembers telling herself through some of her matches, "Just let me get through this. Just be tough." Little did she know at the time that she was being attacked by a disease that affects more women than diabetes or heart attacks.

By making her disease public, Williams hopes to help others who have Sjögren's feel less isolated and scared. Revealing to the world that she has Sjögren's will undoubtedly help alleviate the suffering that millions of people have been enduring. Once in danger of being ignored like PMS, many felt this was simply another woman's disease that needed to stay hidden under the rug.

Unfortunately, there are some doctors who admit they have never heard of it, even though it's a very major disease. Other physicians simply regard it as being trivial. This lack of awareness by the medical community is certainly not deliberate. Sjögren's affects many different organs with overlapping manifestations, which sometimes make it extremely difficult to put all the pieces together in the clinical setting.

If it took her doctors years to finally diagnose her, how would the typical patient ever know this disease exists? "I didn't even know if what I was feeling was the right thing to feel," Venus said. "I don't know anyone else with the disease. When I got the diagnosis, I was like, S-j . . . how do you say it?"

"SHOW-grins," that's how to pronounce it. This incurable disease has changed everything for Williams. "I do the best I can. It's obviously very frustrating; there are a lot of stages to go through with a thing like this, but I have to accept there are people a lot worse off than I am," Venus said. "I haven't gotten to the stage when I ask myself, 'Why me?' I'm still competitive, and I'm not allowed to feel sorry for myself," she added.

Sometimes, simply moving takes a great deal of effort. Her joints creak, and some are misshapen. There are days when she's scared and anxious. Sometimes, she does not want to leave her home. "Rolling the dice," she calls it.

"Every morning is different. Sometimes, I don't feel great then it's a better day than I thought it was going to be. When I wake up, I just have to see how it goes." Williams went on to say, "This is a process I have to learn from working things out for myself and with my doctors. It's almost like beginning again. I have to be positive."

Williams finds it difficult to describe how she feels but has put it this way: "I always tell people it's like going to the races. The other cars are ready. The drivers are prepared. So you have to be more confident than everyone else." That's because Williams is not ready or prepared the way she wants to be because, many times, it hurts tremendously just to move her arms.

After pulling out of the tournament, Venus had to endure a seven-month layoff period. However, even after being zapped of all her energy and stamina, Williams was determined to continue playing tennis. Her sister Serena said, "Everything she's doing is so inspiring for me."

Indeed, everything Venus Williams is doing is very inspiring, not only to people with Sjögren's or any other chronic, incurable disease, but also to people who simply need to be encouraged and uplifted with a sense of hope. She is by far a winner on and off the court.

Although the news may have been devastating when she first learned she has Sjögren's, Williams is determined to fight back and not let this disease win. She has dominated the tennis courts for many years, and her incredible fortitude and resilience will likely play an integral part in this newest competition and her desire to defeat it.

Even before she was diagnosed with this disease, she was told she had exercise-induced asthma. How could this incredible athlete compete at the most stringent level of tennis with asthma? It must be her steadfast desire to be the best she can be, regardless of what physical or health limitations she may encounter. What an inspiration she is to all of us, and what a great sense of hope and awareness she brings to millions of others who are, just now, learning what it truly takes to be a winner.

Chapter 3

What Did My Doctor Say?

WHEN I DECIDED to write this book, I knew I would search for five extraordinary women who have Sjögren's to share their personal stories and testimonies to help encourage others. I knew there would be triumphant stories just waiting to be told that would help encourage others going through the same thing. I set out on a quest to find these incredible survivors who would be willing to share the intimate details of what the journey has been like for them.

It often takes five to seven years on average before being diagnosed. Why so long? Even someone like Venus Williams did not arrive at this confirmation quickly, and I would imagine that she has access to the best doctors in the world.

In my pursuit to tell this story, my desire was to find others who had already been through this who could help inspire others, including me. As aforementioned, I self-diagnosed myself, and I desperately needed some encouragement while I was writing the book and seeking answers to my own medical predicament.

I went to see my primary care physician a few days after reading Venus's announcement and discovering that I had many of the same classic symptoms. My complaints had intensified over the last year or two. It came as no surprise that my doctor referred me to a rheumatologist, but what did surprise me was that I had to wait four and a half months just to see him. Apparently, rheumatologists are in very high demand, and the wait time simply to be seen for an initial consultation can be long and exasperating.

My doctor asked me, "Even if you do have it, then what? Do you really want to be labeled as having it? It's so difficult to get insurance after you've been labeled. And what's worse is that the treatment for it is not specific anyway. There is no cure, so why not just treat the symptoms, regardless of whether you have it or not. Why go through all the trouble and tests, which can be expensive and inconclusive?"

Actually, he was right. Or was he? Why go through all of this simply to find out if I have it or not? Why not just treat the symptoms without having the diagnosis? That's another reason why I am driven to bring about awareness to Sjögren's. Many who suffer from this illness do so in debilitating pain and agonizing silence. Their symptoms are frequently not taken seriously, or they are told that they're simply a little tired or suffering from depression. They look fine, so what could be wrong? It's really not a big deal, is it?

I could have very easily become another silent sufferer, but I wanted answers because I was absolutely convinced that I had the same myriad of symptoms. Thus, my 139-day wait began from the time I saw my primary care physician until my first appointment with the rheumatologist.

As I waited for the appointment date to finally arrive, I continued my research and my mission to find five women willing to share their lives with me. I wondered if it would be as difficult finding these women as getting the diagnosis confirmed. I soon realized there are hundreds, if not thousands, of women who are already out there telling their stories and making a difference. I had no idea but, soon, discovered all I had to do was ask.

Through the Sjögren's Syndrome Foundation, not only was I introduced to a whole new world and wealth of information, but I also was amazed to meet some truly remarkable women who opened their hearts and allowed me to come in. Their compelling stories and unforgettable testimonies will indeed inspire and encourage you, whether you have Sjögren's or not.

Chapter 4

Celebrity Panel

VENUS WILLIAMS IS undeniably a fabulous tennis player, but she's certainly not the typical Sjögren's patient. Well, actually, she is the typical patient because she has to face all the same struggles and battles of uncertainty they all encounter on a daily basis. But, honestly, it's hard for the average person to relate to someone of her celebrityhood because our daily challenges are so much different from this spectacular athlete.

While lending her face and raising awareness of Sjögren's will undoubtedly help others suffering from this chronic and, sometimes, debilitating condition, Williams is to be highly commended for offering hope and inspiring others.

Although the five women you are about to meet are not celebrities per se, I will refer to them as my celebrity panel. The definition of a celebrity is a person who has a prominent profile and commands a great deal of public fascination and influence. The term is synonymous with wealth, implied with great popular appeal, prominent in a particular field, and is easily recognized by the general public.

Whereas people may indeed gain celebrity status as a result of a successful career in a particular field, in other cases, people become celebrities due to media attention for their extravagant lifestyle or wealth or for their connections to famous people.

Although these five women do not technically possess those attributes, they definitely define the face of Sjögren's. In my opinion, they are the epitome of success because they have met this challenge head-on, and they are winning the battle. They absolutely personify extravagant lifestyles simply because they have learned to live without something even wealth cannot buy, and that's good health. My celebrity panel is the quintessence of prominence in the often-misunderstood world of silent Sjögren's sufferers.

Yes, Venus Williams is by far the most renowned Sjögren's patient in the world. The Sjögren's community is deeply gratified by the awareness she has brought to this disease. But it's time to meet five everyday women who were thrust into the same playing field as Williams long before she caused such a media frenzy making "Show Grins" a household name. Quite frankly, it is still not a household name, and most Americans still do not know it even exists.

In January 2012, the Sjögren's Syndrome Foundation was proud to announce that an aggressive five-year breakthrough goal was set that will change the face of Sjögren's. The goal is to shorten the time to diagnose Sjögren's by 50% in five years.

Let's meet Cathy, Estrella, Judy, Lynn, and Paula to see if they can help speed this up a bit more than that. These five celebrities are to, indeed, be commended for sharing their remarkable journeys and changing the face of Sjögren's. When you walk alongside each one of them to hear their individual stories, you will find yourself living inside their testimonies with them.

Cathy Taylor

Chapter 5

Seven Weeks Instead
of Seven Years

ALTHOUGH ARRIVING AT a Sjögren's diagnosis is often an exhaustive, five-to-seven-year tedious journey, there are cases discovered much more quickly. It's not the norm, but in Cathy's case, she is one of very few who was diagnosed before she even realized she was having symptoms. As the second eldest of five siblings, born in East Greenbush, New York, Cathy's childhood in no way prepared her for what was to surface fifty years later.

Three years prior to Cathy's birth, Japan surrendered, prompting the end of World War II in 1945. President Franklin D. Roosevelt died in office on the twelfth day of April that same year and was succeeded by Vice President Harry S. Truman. Adolf Hitler committed suicide eighteen days later in his Berlin bunker.

Cathy's teenage parents had no idea what the future would hold for their bouncing baby girl born in 1948 when Truman was President. Cathy was the couple's second daughter born a mere fourteen months after her elder sister. Her parents were but children themselves during the war, and as teen parents of two baby girls during the late 1940's, they simply did the best they could. Remarkably, Cathy's childhood was totally uneventful, and she was unaware of the historically significant time period in which she was born.

Fast-forward to Cathy Taylor, wife and mother of two sons, nothing about her past medical history would indicate that trouble lay ahead. Things remained uneventful for Cathy. She was asymptomatic and lived a very busy, active lifestyle. Of course, she dreamed that her children would grow up and accomplish great things one day. Mothers teach their children that they can do anything they set their minds to if they work hard, including finding the cure for incurable diseases. Was that something Cathy instilled in her son, Steven Taylor?

It wasn't until both of her children were grown did Cathy have the first notion that something was awry. Her sister had come over for a visit and informed Cathy that she had some type of growth or mass in her throat. She asked Cathy to feel her throat, the same area of your neck most physicians feel when you go in for a checkup. Cathy felt a mass in her sister's throat. She then felt her own throat, and, just like her sister, Cathy's throat also had a lump.

After seeing an endocrinologist, Cathy's sister was informed that she had goiter, which was swelling of her thyroid gland. No surgery was needed. As fate would have it, Cathy already had an upcoming appointment scheduled with her gynecologist for a routine annual exam. She mentioned the lump in her throat, and, upon examining Cathy, he told her that she needed to see a specialist and that the growth would likely need to be removed. Cathy was prepared for the worst as she was informed by the surgeon that, in 99% of cases like hers, the mass would be cancerous.

Cathy planned for surgery with almost certainty that she would be diagnosed with cancer, but, amazingly, the surgeon only had to remove one half of her thyroid gland. The sample was sent to the lab where they later confirmed that Cathy was in the minority one percent. She did not have cancer. Incredibly, Cathy never knew anything was wrong prior to this. She had no symptoms, and it wasn't until her sister discovered that she had goiter did Cathy even seek medical treatment after realizing she also had a mass in her neck.

Totally unaffected by the first time she had to seek any sort of medical treatment other than for routine exams, Cathy simply continued her very active lifestyle. A year after thyroid surgery, an inconsequential pinkeye diagnosis would begin a very surprising chain of events. Her incredibly red eyes and severe eye pain yielded a pinkeye diagnosis and routine medication. A couple of weeks later, her eyes hurt so badly that she had to go to the emergency room over the weekend, and again she was diagnosed with pinkeye. The medication the second time around made it even worse, and she could barely see.

It was December, and Cathy needed to go Christmas shopping. She didn't have time for all of this, so she pushed herself and kept going. By this time, she had noticed in addition to the severe eye pain, her fingers and toes had begun to hurt, perhaps due to the cold weather. The pain was intermittent, but, at times, it hurt so badly that she could barely touch anything. As she was shopping with her husband, Joe, his chivalry was in full swing because this gentleman had to open the doors for Cathy. She was in too much pain to even open the door for herself.

Four weeks from when she had the first bout with pinkeye, it returned for the third time. At least, she had survived the Christmas holiday season, but this was really getting ridiculous. Once or twice, perhaps, but by the third time, her doctor knew there had to be something else wrong, so he did other tests. Cathy went home thinking she simply had the most awful luck of any fifty-year-old suffering from what is typically a kiddie disease.

It was on a beautiful, sunny Sunday afternoon when Cathy received the phone call from her doctor. Immediately, she knew it had to be more serious than pinkeye. No doctor calls a patient on a Sunday afternoon to talk about pinkeye.

"Hello, Cathy. This is Dr. Teitgens. Do you have a minute?" Of course, Cathy anxiously replied, "Yes."

"Have you ever heard of lupus?" Of course, her answer was yes again, although she really didn't know what it was, but, like most people, Cathy had at least heard of lupus.

She went in for more tests and hurried out thinking to herself that she needs to simply get a diagnosis and get on with her life. If it's lupus, then so be it. If it's not, then she wanted her doctor to hurry and find out what it was because she just had too much to do and didn't have time to be sick.

Cathy remembers thinking, "I don't care what I have. I need to get on with my life. Of course, I'm going to have some aches and pains, and, of course, I'm going to be more fatigued at fifty than I was at thirty."

Cathy didn't understand what was really going on but proceeded to make an appointment with the rheumatologist she was referred to. Her X-rays had come back negative, but her blood work did confirm she had some type of autoimmune disease. Being void of any apparent symptoms, she wondered if she really did have lupus.

In spite of what occurred over the Christmas season a few weeks prior with the severe pain in her fingers and toes, Cathy was still under the assumption that her body was going through a change anyway at this age, and there was no reason to be whining about not feeling as well as she did when she was younger.

Within a seven week time frame, from her first symptoms of what she thought was a simple case of pinkeye to blood work at Dr. Lee Shapiro's office in Albany, New York, the mystery was solved. "Cathy, you have Sjögren's syndrome. Have you ever heard of that?" he asked.

"No." But whatever it was, Cathy simply thought she would continue life as usual. After all, she had no real symptoms that she knew of. Even though this graduate of Yale University and Columbia University School of Medicine had been practicing rheumatology since 1982, Dr. Shapiro's diagnosis of Cathy in 1998 basically did not mean a great deal to her. She still felt pretty good for a woman her age and didn't think this autoimmune disease would impact her very busy life. She made no plans to slow down.

She went home and told her family that she had Sjögren's. They thought it was a very minor thing and didn't give it much thought at all. How bad could it be? A few weeks prior, she had pinkeye. Seven weeks later, she had Sjögren's. Cathy didn't want her family to worry, so she didn't dwell on it either. It was time for her to get on with her life, so back to riding horses and ballroom dancing she went.

Soon, Cathy realized it wasn't life as usual. Symptoms she had previously ignored became apparent. She couldn't walk on her toes anymore, but she could still ride horses. When Cathy rode, it was on the balls of her feet, which meant, she could still participate in the horse riding competitions that she loved. It didn't matter that once she got off the horse, she could barely walk. Sometimes, her husband would even have to help carry her off to the side after she finished the competition because she literally could not walk due to the pain.

Cathy's philosophy: "Life is a dance. The steps are simply going to change."

Chapter 6

The Change of Life

MANY PEOPLE REFER to menopause as "going through the change" or "the change of life." It usually occurs when women reach their late forties or early fifties. But what happens when you are fifty years old and suddenly discover that you may have to go through two different changes simultaneously?

Cathy had expected menopause to occur around a certain age, like it does for all women. It's somewhat of a rite of passage as you realize middle age has really set in, and you're just not going to feel as good as you did when you were younger. There's no mystery about it. It's a normal part of womanhood that we all must face.

What she didn't expect was to suddenly become symptomatic of something far worse, a chronic autoimmune disease with no cure. At least with menopause, you endure until it's over because you know eventually it will be over, and you'll come out on the other side.

With Sjögren's, there is no end. It's a chronic condition that you must simply learn to live with, and that's exactly what Cathy did. How frustrating it must have been though to live with a disease no one had ever heard of. She couldn't even pronounce it correctly, and her family thought no more of it than pinkeye initially.

As Cathy began to research this newfound condition, she began to realize she was likely symptomatic many years prior to being diagnosed. Although she didn't associate dry mouth as anything significant, she recognized that she had suffered from dental issues dating back to her twenties, most likely due to Sjögren's.

"Cathy, you really need to take better care of your teeth." How embarrassing it was every time her dentist told her that. "Cathy, are you brushing and flossing every day?" How insulting to be questioned about proper dental hygiene when she knew she meticulously cared for her teeth, yet she constantly faced dental issues. Root canal after root canal, but nothing seemed to work. After all her teeth had undergone root canals, she still had problems. The next step was to proceed with caps on her teeth.

Unfortunately, since dry mouth was the adversary, her dentist failed to realize the caps weren't going to work either. Her mouth was simply too dry, and nothing was going to work. "Cathy, you really need to take better care of your teeth." Those were meaningless words because Cathy had taken better care of her teeth than the majority of the population. But, alas, she was unaware that no matter what she did, until the dry mouth issue was addressed, she would constantly be insulted by dentists who never knew to associate dry mouth as the root of her dental problems.

As it is with so many Sjögren's patients, isolated symptoms didn't mean anything because no one was looking at the big picture. For nearly thirty years, Cathy had undergone belittling comments from well-meaning dentists who never knew she was exhibiting one of the classic hallmark symptoms of Sjögren's. What a costly oversight on everyone's part.

Even though Cathy thought she had been diagnosed with a minor condition for which she had no symptoms, further reflections told a much different story. In addition to the dental issues, Cathy realized the trouble she had been having with her fingers and toes was also related to Sjögren's. No wonder she couldn't open the door at the shopping mall.

She also had an explanation now as to why she frequently felt so very tired with no stamina at all. It wasn't that she was going through the change, although she was certainly going through a change. As hard as she tried, she realized she really couldn't continue life as usual. She refused to give up ballroom dancing and competitive horseback riding though. She refused to settle into middle age with the stamina of an old woman. She also refused to tell anyone other than her family that she had Sjögren's.

"Why don't you just do less, Cathy? Then you won't be so tired." Her well-meaning friends thought it was merely time to give up some things and make some lifestyle changes. "Cathy, if riding horses makes your feet hurt, then stop riding. Do something else, and you won't hurt." Obviously, her friends thought the solution lay within Cathy herself. All she had to do was make some minor adjustments in her life, and all her complaints and problems would go away. Surely, Sjögren's was not going to negatively impact this vivacious woman.

For about eight years after her diagnosis, Cathy kept quiet because no one really believed she was sick anyway. It wasn't too much for her to handle. She could deal with the symptoms and continue working in various administrative type positions while enjoying a very busy social life as well. Sjögren's was not going to stop her.

One day, Cathy decided it was time to speak up. She didn't want to keep quiet anymore. She had accepted the fact that she would have to adjust to the chronic nature of this disease. The symptoms would never go away, but she most certainly could learn to adapt and make some healthy changes. She decided it wasn't good to keep quiet, not even about a very personal aspect of this disease . . . dry vagina.

How could this vibrant, outgoing, effervescent woman admit that she not only suffered from dry eyes and dry mouth, but also from dry vagina? Shhh, those are hush words that definitely don't need to be discussed in mixed company, let alone in this inspirational book. Her own dentist had failed to associate thirty years of tooth decay to Sjögren's. Surely, Cathy wasn't blaming Sjögren's for these other "*difficulties*" in a much more private area.

Au contraire! Not only did Cathy realize her dry vagina was caused by this autoimmune disease that attacked her moisture-producing glands, but she even had the audacity to make others talk about it as well. Being the outspoken person that she is, Cathy took it upon herself to bring up this issue at Sjögren's conferences.

Imagine this grandmother of six opening up a conversation about a very confidential topic. She stood on stage at the conference and opened up by stating, "Today, I'm going to talk about dry vagina." As you can imagine, she brought the house down. Cathy's take on things: "It's just a fact of life. It is what it is." Needless to say, everyone at the conference listening to her speech had something to talk about when they went home.

Surprisingly, Cathy's own rheumatologist was at this conference and didn't even know that Cathy had dry vagina. She never told him. Because the hallmark symptoms are dry eyes and dry mouth, Dr. Shapiro only asked Cathy about those two areas. As most rheumatologists would do when assessing a person for the first time for an autoimmune disease, the vagina topic simply did not make it to the conversation.

It was several years after her initial meeting with Dr. Shapiro that Cathy decided to take a very public stage to talk about dry vagina for the first time. It goes without saying that every time Dr. Shapiro sees a new patient now, he asks them about dry eyes, dry mouth, and dry vagina. It really does help formulate a diagnosis much more quickly in some cases.

As with most things related to Sjögren's, awareness is crucial, and, until people are aware of the possible symptoms, they never put the big picture together and often suffer for years on end with no help. No, there is no magical blue pill to take, but there are ways to try to minimize the symptoms and obtain a better quality of life.

If you don't recognize that you have a medical condition that is causing physical symptoms, you may find yourself suffering needlessly. If left untreated, the condition could intensify and affect vital organs. That's why it is so important to talk about it, even if it's an uncomfortable topic.

Cathy's willingness to open the lines of communication and force people to talk about all areas of dryness, not just the eyes and mouth, has helped countless women and their partners face this otherwise secret symptom of a silent disease. Even though Cathy was good at talking about it, she didn't shop for it. When it was time to purchase products to help the dryness, she sent her husband to the pharmacy. Cathy laughed and said, "What did he care? Everyone would know the items weren't for him anyway."

After breaking the ice about the unspoken symptom, Cathy has also challenged other Sjögren's patients to think outside the box. "You have to reinvent yourself after the diagnosis." That was good advice Cathy offered other patients at a Sjögren's conference.

During one of her roundtable open discussions, she presented the topic: *Reinventing Yourself after the Diagnosis.* "You may need to make a change in your life because you may not be able to do all the activities you once did. Find other areas of interest and pursue activities that are within your new normal." This was excellent advice to women facing this life-altering diagnosis. It simply can't be business as usual because you don't have the same body as usual.

"Perhaps you may need to take up a different hobby such as knitting." Good advice? Well that depends on who you ask. Cathy suggested this to a group of women at a Sjögren's conference, and it seemed well received. It wasn't until she got the conference evaluation forms afterward that Cathy realized she had disappointed one of the participants.

"I didn't want to hear about knitting at a Sjögren's conference. I came here for help." What this conference attendee failed to realize was that was the help she needed. Sure, she could have learned a lot from the other panel of physicians and autoimmune experts, but she also needed practical advice. She needed to understand this is a lifelong condition and how well you accept the changes and learn to live with it affects your entire well-being.

Don't be fooled into thinking you can do everything as you once did because the disease will undoubtedly affect many different aspects of your overall well-being. It's monumental that you realize you must go through a change.

Cathy's intention was purely to help others realize Sjögren's is never going away, so perhaps you need to look at doing something you never did before. Maybe some attendees were not open to this suggestion and were looking for the miracle pill, which simply does not exist.

Just as beauty is in the eye of the beholder, help is often closer than you think. No, there is no cure. But there is certainly a great deal of help available. Learning to live with a chronic illness is a lifelong challenge, and Cathy's desire is to share her story with others to improve their quality of life. Cathy has changed. Obviously, she's not the same fifty-year-old who thought she had pinkeye. Instead, she is the perfect example of learning to live with something you may not have even known you had.

Chapter 7

A Family Affair

CATHY WASN'T THE only one in her family who made a change. One of her sons was working for the American Heart Association when a head hunter contacted him about applying for the chief executive officer (CEO) position at the Sjögren's Syndrome Foundation. Being very excited about the possible career move, Steven called Cathy to tell her about the forthcoming interview. She wasn't home when he called, so he told Joe instead. Much to Steven's surprise, Joe told him, "Your mother has Sjögren's."

"What?" Why was Steven surprised? Cathy had informed her family the same day Dr. Shapiro diagnosed her in 1998. But what she didn't tell them was how to properly pronounce it. At the time, Cathy had allowed her children and the rest of the family to think it was a very minor condition like pinkeye. They really didn't talk about it, and when they did, Steven never knew she was referring to Sjögren's because she didn't know she was mispronouncing it.

When Cathy was teaching her young sons that they could one day do anything they set their minds to, little did she know that one of them may grow up and help find the cure for her incurable disease. Steven went to the job interview and has been CEO of the Sjögren's Syndrome Foundation for almost a decade now. Awareness is critical, and he has played an integral part in increasing awareness about this disease, which, for years, he never even knew his mother had.

At one of the fundraising and awareness events, Cathy was running in the Turkey Trot in New York with four of her grandkids. A young woman in her twenties saw them all wearing "Team Sjögren's" T-shirt, and her eyes lit up. "I have Sjögren's . . . I have Sjögren's."

This young woman who was running the Turkey Trot for a different reason was inspired to see Cathy and her grandchildren running for the same disease she had. Cathy proceeded to tell her about the foundation, and, a few months later, this same twenty-something-year-old was running in the half-marathon in Nashville to increase awareness and help raise funds.

After finally coming to terms with her own diagnosis and changing her lifestyle accordingly, Cathy discovered it was much easier to live with a silent disease by making it public. She mistakenly allowed her family to believe it was insignificant as she attempted to mask the symptoms she didn't even realize she had initially.

These days, it's a family affair with her husband, Joe, two children, and six grandchildren, ages six to nineteen. Living with a chronic illness requires acceptance of the disease, and it's much easier if you have a support system who understands.

Cathy has continued to work professionally while volunteering for the foundation as well. Even though extreme fatigue is still a very major component that can be debilitating, she paces herself and gets it all done. As the assistant director of the New School Center for Media in Albany, Cathy helps students embark upon every aspect of a career in electronic and broadcast media.

Her incredible drive to organize and help others was immediately recognized by the school. She is truly a dynamo with unwavering passion to help people and make things work. As a professional, she is dedicated to the students she serve and to their success, which exemplifies the true spirit of the school.

On the entertainment side, Cathy is currently a producer for both the Miss California and Miss New York components of the Miss USA Pageant. Along with organizing and directing various businesses for more than two decades, Cathy has worked as a writer for a Kentucky-based magazine, the *Bluegrass Horseman*.

It is that same passion and desire from her professional life that carries over to her volunteer work for Sjögren's. In 2011, she was featured in an article by the *New York Times* for her work with the Sjögren's Syndrome Foundation which included organizing a Lunafest where they showed short films written by women about women's issues to raise funds.

At the end of the day, Cathy is sometimes so fatigued that her husband has to help her to bed. It's not the typical fatigue or low stamina but this totally overwhelming feeling of absolute exhaustion that simply cannot be put into words. However, she gets up the next day and starts all over again because she is passionate and committed to helping others learn to live their best lives possible with this grossly misunderstood disease.

Yes, there are days when the joint pain and fatigue seem too much to bear, but she keeps going and planning for the next half-marathon. Remaining silent did not work for Cathy. She has way too much to say. She strives to put Sjögren's in the forefront by participating in numerous local, regional, and national events every year.

Cathy's desire is to help others not only understand the disease but learn how to live a better and more fulfilled life with it. She is a beautiful, physically fit grandmother in her sixties who was diagnosed with Sjögren's at age fifty. She's still running half-marathon events across the country from New York to California and everywhere in between. Although ballroom dancing is yet her passion, running is her personal challenge and family tradition now.

She encourages others to find out as much as they can about Sjögren's by any means necessary. She stresses the importance of learning at your own level based on how you comprehend new things. If you like to talk and be around other people, support groups would be very helpful. If you prefer to read, there are many books about Sjögren's that would be beneficial. If you like to research and search the internet, there is a wealth of information on the Sjögren's Syndrome Foundation website, Sjogrens.org.

The point is, whatever your method of learning is, gather all the information you can and make the necessary changes in your life. Find a doctor who is knowledgeable of the disease and understands what you are going through. Take control of your situation, and learn how to live your life to the fullest.

Although Cathy didn't realize, as a young girl, the significant time period in which she was born, she has made a bit of history herself as she leads by example. She took her own advice and changed her steps. She's still dancing, and, now, others can follow in her footsteps. She isn't a paid spokesperson, but she certainly looks and sounds as if she could be. And that is why she is the first celebrity on this panel!

Estrella Bibbey

Chapter 8

Born to Be a Republican

WHAT BETTER PLACE for hippies to live during the late 1960s and early 1970s than in between Albuquerque and Santa Fe, New Mexico. Estrella's parents were back-to-the-land organic gardeners living on Sun Farm, a hippie commune. Their one-room adobe hut wasn't exactly the ideal place to give birth, but that was the plan for these free-spirited parents-to-be.

Baby Estrella had different plans though, insisting that she be delivered in a real hospital. As she puts it, she insisted on being a republican even before she was born by presenting in the breech position prior to birth. Since this was not the type of delivery that could be performed safely at the commune, her parents had to go to the hospital anyway. That was the only way for this self-preserving, baby republican to secure her real birth certificate.

The first few years of her life began on a beach living out of a blue Ford van on the Yucatán Peninsula. As a toddler, Estrella was pulling and eating carrots and radishes right out of the garden. She remembers picking rose hips with her mother by the creek when she was four years old, but things changed dramatically when her parents moved to western Oregon when she was six.

It was in Oregon that she entered a public school for the very first time, and then Estrella's former-hippie parents enrolled her in a local Catholic school a short time later. Things normalized in her life, and the apparent Type A personality soon began to shine.

While making the transition from the hippie commune to Catholic schools in Oregon, Estrella's parents also changed. Her mother went to college when Estrella was in high school, obtained a degree in journalism, and became a technical writer for a software company. Interestingly, her grandparents also had careers in journalism dating back to the 1940s.

As a female news writer during that time period, Estrella's grandmother set the precedent for the rest of the females in her family to follow. Her grandfather ran a printing press, and, with those skills, he and Estrella's grandmother would travel to different cities and buy the local newspapers to run. Even her mother's brother followed this same career path and worked for the *Indianapolis Star* his entire career as a sports writer until he retired.

It was apparent that Estrella would also follow this same path, and her identity soon became her career. Being more of a visual person, Estrella majored in journalism in college and became an extremely successful photojournalist. It's who she was, and her life could never have gone any other way.

While in college, Estrella met Jerry Bibbey, who went on to become a golf course superintendent after obtaining his degree in turf management. Thus, the charmed life began for Jerry and Estrella. What a cute young couple with very promising careers. This simply solidified who she was, and her entire identity was immersed in her career. Jerry's career moved them from Oregon to Norman, Oklahoma where Estrella secured a staff photographer position with one of the larger newspapers in Oklahoma, the *Norman Transcript*. She won numerous awards for her work there and was often given huge double page spreads to run her extensive picture stories.

The young couple relocated to Long Island, New York where the charmed lifestyle went into full force. Having the confidence of a much more seasoned and established photojournalist, Estrella's self-assurance and poise took her straight to *Newsday*, the largest newspaper on Long Island. She convinced them that this girl with an Oklahoma newspaper background was ready for the major league with this New York newspaper. They brought her on, initially, as a freelancer.

She made connections in New York and freelanced for magazines there, as well as in New Jersey and Connecticut. By this time, she was working much more than full time. Estrella's life was her work, and she had already made a name for herself in the business by the time she was in her mid-twenties.

Six months after moving to New York, Estrella suddenly found herself not feeling well but didn't stop working long enough to see what was wrong. She simply pressed on and continued working for about a month because she was too busy to think about taking care of herself. At the advice of a friend, she finally sought medical treatment with her primary care physician, and after literally dragging herself into her office with a fever of 104 degrees, Estrella found herself having an emergency appendectomy a short two hours later.

Stunned at his discovery, the surgeon found scar tissue on her appendix where it had ruptured and attempted to heal over the past month. Complications arose, and she developed peritonitis, an infection of the lining in her abdomen. At the age of twenty-seven, Estrella found herself quite ill, and it's still a wonder how she had maintained such a grueling work schedule for all that time leading up to the emergency surgery.

This was the beginning of what was to come three to six months later. Estrella returned to work, totally engulfed in her career once again. She was as busy as ever and certainly didn't have time to stop and be sick. Because she worked so much, she simply thought she was dehydrated. She didn't know that her dry mouth was the first sign of Sjögren's. She traveled with a case of water in her trunk and gum in her camera bag.

Being unaware that dry mouth is actually a medical condition, she never sought treatment for it. Estrella simply continued working and told no one. It didn't matter that food had started to stick to her tongue, teeth, and lips or that certain foods caused a burning sensation in her mouth.

It was about three years later, after she and Jerry had relocated to California, when she noticed she was having seasonal allergies which she attributed to the new environment. Estrella started taking allergy shots while her body adjusted from the New York air to California air. During her treatment for the allergies, she went into anaphylactic shock on two separate occasions.

After the second time the allergist had to save her life, she knew it was much more than seasonal allergies. Having an immunology background, this well-informed allergy specialist knew to run an autoimmune blood panel, and, with that very simple blood test, Estrella was instantly diagnosed with Sjögren's in 2003.

Her doctor very seriously and somewhat gravely explained it to her, but Estrella didn't think anything of it. She rushed out of the doctor's office and went back to work that same day thinking her doctor was just a very serious and grave person. She didn't really need to seek further medical care with a rheumatologist, did she? Sjögren's couldn't be that bad, could it?

Estrella continued working but became more aware that she did indeed have dry mouth, dry eyes, joint pain, and fatigue. She had ignored those symptoms for quite some time, but after googling Sjögren's and learning more about it, it was apparent that she was exhibiting all the classic symptoms. None of this stopped her from working because she was engulfed in the family tradition of being defined by her career.

Explaining her symptoms away, Estrella thought the dry mouth was due to dehydration, and the dry eyes was due to seasonal allergies. All she needed to do was to get more exercise and take more vitamins, and, surely, the fatigue and joint pain would go away. And even though she didn't have a repetitive-motion-type job, Estrella had already undergone bilateral carpal tunnel surgery prior to this. At the time of her surgery, the orthopedic specialist never saw the big picture. He never realized the numbness she was experiencing in her hands prior to surgery had been caused by Sjögren's.

Ingrained in the belief that work is the most important aspect of one's life, Estrella's attitude was that no matter what, her career was more important than anything else. Her mother encouraged her to continue working no matter what. Illness just was not an option. Being healthy in this family was paramount, so, obviously, Estrella had to press onward and upward as if she was completely well. But she wasn't . . .

Chapter 9

Lack of Reaction Leads
to Surprising Action

AS ESTRELLA TOLD her family and friends and got their emotionless reaction and lack of sympathy about her diagnosis, Estrella's attitude imitated theirs. They basically had no reaction to the news and essentially thought nothing was wrong, so Estrella made up her mind to respond in the same nonchalant manner.

No one said, "Oh my gosh, that's so horrible. That's really going to change your life."

Their biggest question was simply if she had AIDS/HIV because they had confused the terminology autoimmune disease and immunodeficiency disease. After assuring them she had Sjögren's, not AIDS/HIV, most of Estrella's family, friends, and acquaintances thought nothing more of it. For the next one and a half years, Estrella continued working as if nothing was wrong because no one treated her as if anything was wrong. Surely, she wasn't really sick after all.

Estrella was in excruciating pain, and her ability to function went downhill very rapidly. She went from being a healthy young wife of twenty-seven to a very dependent and ill woman. At the end of a work day, after carrying the heavy camera equipment all day and driving back home, she could barely get out of the car and stand up. There were times her husband would have to literally come out to the car to assist her into the house. This incredibly driven professional photojournalist soon became an incredibly sick woman.

The inflammation and joint pain had gotten so bad that she couldn't even raise her arms to wash her hair anymore. Simple activities of daily living became impossible to accomplish. Because she was having all these difficulties, her doctors prescribed different medications to alleviate the drastic symptoms. Unfortunately, Estrella was forced to react differently. She could no longer ignore the obvious.

The weight of the camera and lenses while trying to shoot pictures became absolutely unbearable. Her fingers, hands, wrists, arms, elbows, and shoulders hurt terribly. She could no longer grab the always-ready, forty-pound camera bag and hit the ground running whenever she received a telephone call about a news story she was to photograph. In actuality, Estrella couldn't really grab anything and go. It was all beyond her physical ability, and she had to make a painful decision.

Estrella had to give up her career as an accomplished and well-respected photojournalist. She was forced to lose her identity. In fact, Sjögren's had theoretically stolen her identity.

At the time, she was working for a conglomerate of newspapers in the San Francisco Bay area, and she couldn't even bring herself to tell them the truth. In total denial and afraid to admit that she was sick, Estrella resigned from her position in 2005. She told her photo editor she was leaving because she wanted a position that had been offered to someone else. This was easier than explaining she was sick with a disease no one had ever heard of or could even pronounce.

But, of course, Estrella wasn't fit for any position, not even her own. However, being unable to accept the fact that she was simply too sick to continue working, it was much more convenient for her to blame something else. She left the newspaper without anyone even knowing she had Sjögren's.

Estrella went home to a place where she had never been before. She had worked her entire adulthood in a profession she loved. It was most bizarre to be in this frightening position of uncertainty. Emotionally, it was extremely difficult for her to even admit that she was ill. She had no reason to be at home, but, all of a sudden, she found herself trying to explain to others why she no longer worked. In spite of everything, Estrella had always been identified by her career and her dream jobs. It is who she was. Now that she no longer had a career, she felt she had no identity either.

"I'm retired due to illness." What an odd way of attempting to explain to people why she no longer worked. She became very awkward in social situations, and this once-confident, highly driven, extremely competitive and successful photojournalist was compelled to hide the truth.

Fortunately, Jerry was doing very well in his career as a turf manager. Estrella began to spend more time golfing even though she was physically unable to walk the course. She adapted by riding in a golf cart and was still exhausted after only playing nine holes. It was through Jerry's work that she met and became close friends with Ruth, a golf course general manager who had been diagnosed with Multiple Sclerosis (MS) three years prior. Her life had been turned upside down because of the MS, so she could definitely relate to Estrella and offer her words of wisdom and encouragement. It was as if God had put this dear friend in Estrella's life to help her through a very dark period.

Ruth became an unexpected but amazing guide for Estrella. Prior to this time, Estrella had not experienced much in terms of spiritual growth and maturity. For her entire life, she had done nothing but work, so she never took time to truly analyze her life to figure out what was really important. Her new friend helped her to evaluate her own life. Estrella realized that the over-achieving Type A personality she once was had not actually netted her very much in terms of true happiness. For the first time, she realized all she had done her entire life was devote herself to her job.

After she was able to reflect on her life and understand the high level of stress she had grown accustomed to functioning during the ten years that she was a highly competitive photojournalist, Estrella was happy to finally be able to slow down and think about who she was for the very first time.

Jerry and Estrella began to travel overseas to exotic places in Europe and visited friends in England. She accepted the fact that she could no longer work and ultimately completed the process of applying for disability. As depressing as it was to be approved, it further validated the fact that she needed to be at home instead of work, but that in itself was an upsetting notion. Although Estrella knew she was no longer able to work, being certified on paper as being disabled was not a comforting thought at the time. It was challenging and difficult for her to accept being told she really was sick and had a bona fide disability.

Not long after accepting the fact that she did have an identity outside of her career, Estrella and Jerry put together a team of doctors and health care professionals that they felt would be able to help them in another area of their lives. They wanted to have a baby, but that would not be an easy task.

They had been married for eleven years and were well aware of the genetic mitochondrial disease Estrella carried, which causes blindness in adult male children at an extremely alarming rate. One of Estrella's half-brothers was blind, and, as the female carrier, Estrella knew that if she had a male child, he would almost definitely suffer from this mitochondrial disease.

Being young and impetuous, Estrella and Jerry wanted everything in life, including having their own child. Although she had been advised by her doctors that being pregnant with Sjögren's may be quite detrimental to her health, she wanted to pursue all of her options anyway. There was a time when most Sjögren's patients were diagnosed after their childbearing years, so there was not much research on how Sjögren's affects a woman during pregnancy. She was well aware that there would be many risks and potential complications. Combine Sjögren's with being a mitochondrial disease carrier and therein laid the problem Estrella faced.

Although they agonized for years over the idea of even considering having a baby, it took the Bibbeys one year to conceive. However, this was merely the beginning of Estrella's personal trauma.

Chapter 10

Oh Boy!

ATTEMPTING WITHIN THEIR moral scope and Catholic faith to conceive a child who would not suffer from the mitochondrial disease Estrella carried meant the Bibbeys explored many options to try to ensure having a baby girl. Only a male child would have to face all the health challenges of the genetic disease. The more invasive therapies were ruled out because they went against what they believed in spiritually. Other fertility options were not viable alternatives for Estrella because of Sjögren's.

They could have invested thousands and thousands of dollars to try to circumvent a potential disaster, but they had no guarantees that anything would actually work. To even try to guarantee having a baby girl would have been quite expensive and could have still resulted in a very disappointing outcome emotionally and financially. After exhausting many alternatives, they simply proceeded by faith and hoped the Lord would bless them with a daughter. Regardless of the outcome, Jerry and Estrella believed that no matter what happened with the pregnancy, God would bless them with exactly what they could handle.

One of the first challenges was to find a perinatologist who would be willing to take on her care as a high-risk pregnancy due to the Sjögren's. Not that any obstetrician's job is routine, but, in Estrella's case, the obstetrician would have to specialize even further within the perinatologist subspecialty in order to adequately manage her pregnancy. Quite naturally, because Estrella was in the San Francisco Bay area in California, she looked to Stanford University for help, and there she found her team of highly specialized physicians.

The Lucile Packard Children's Hospital is a world-class, nonprofit hospital devoted entirely to the care of babies, children, adolescents, and expectant mothers. It is an academic medical center on the campus of Stanford University recognized as much for its achievements as for its commitment to care. Estrella was in very good hands at this internationally recognized facility.

It's imperative to stress at this juncture that experts advise all women with Sjögren's who are planning to get pregnant as well as those who have suffered miscarriages to be tested for antibodies. An autoantibody found in women with Sjögren's can very rarely be associated with neonatal lupus in newborns or congenital heart block, an abnormality of the rate or rhythm of the baby's heart. If a heart block is detected, medications or an early delivery may be necessary. In rare cases, antibodies have been associated with recurrent miscarriages as well.

Generally speaking, Sjögren's is likely to flare after delivery as well; therefore, mothers may need to take medication at the time of delivery and for a few weeks afterward to control the flare-ups. Although complications may arise, the vast majority of women with Sjögren's have babies with no congenital abnormalities, but it is vitally important to speak to your physician about possible complications even before you consider having a baby.

While most expectant parents anxiously await an ultrasound, which would show if they would have a boy or girl, Estrella knew she would have the ultrasound at a much earlier stage. It was paramount to know if she was having a boy because of the mitochondrial disease. The day came very early on in the pregnancy. Estrella and Jerry watched other exuberant parents-to-be leaving the office with their one little ultrasound picture. All appeared happy and relieved to know what they were having, although it really didn't matter for the vast majority of parents there if it was a boy or girl.

That would not be the case for the Bibbeys. Instead of one little ultrasound picture so they could be on their merry way, they were given what appeared to be mounds and mounds of pictures and paperwork as they were escorted into a private consultation room. Behind that door, they met with many people in white coats who were prepared to explain to them what the male fetus diagnosis meant.

Yes, it was a diagnosis. There was no joy after their ultrasound. There was no excitement. There was only the feeling of impending doom. They had tried to hold on to a dash of hope, but after being told she would pass on the mitochondrial disease to her baby boy, the entire situation became very medical. Her pregnancy would not be like the fairytale pictures she had seen in all those idealistic pregnancy magazines.

Estrella felt abandoned by God and absolutely devastated. These were indeed the darkest days of her faith. She had been under the belief that God would take care of her and give her everything she wanted, including having a perfectly healthy daughter. Instead, Estrella received telephone calls from social workers asking if she was sure she wanted to continue the pregnancy. What a horribly challenging and dark period in life Estrella had to face.

Mad at God and the rest of the world, Estrella felt all alone and unable to connect with anyone or anything on any level of faith. During one of the follow up phone calls from a social worker, she found herself in a discussion she was horrified to be in. At the very lowest point in her life, Estrella was offered something which they said could actually make it look like "God did it," and no one would ever have to know. Estrella refused.

The pregnancy was far from typical. During the first three weeks, Estrella lost twenty-seven pounds due to an extreme version of morning sickness. She was very ill throughout the pregnancy, not necessarily all due to Sjögren's, but it certainly made matters worse.

She was unable to take the majority of her Sjögren's medications while pregnant, so the symptoms gravely intensified. She was in total misery. Joint pain became almost unbearable, and she faced many challenging moments throughout the pregnancy because treatment of her Sjögren's was so extremely limited due to the potential risks to the baby.

As the pregnancy proceeded, Estrella endured many trials and tribulations. Her doctors were very busy monitoring both the mother and baby in an attempt to avoid a catastrophic ending. She was fortunate enough to circumvent many of the known Sjögren's complications. However, during a routine growth scan test at thirty-seven weeks, which happened to be the day before Mother's Day, 2008, the doctors discovered there was no change in growth from the prior two weeks, which meant a terrible crisis was at hand.

After further testing, Estrella's doctors made a startling discovery. Her embryonic fluid had totally disappeared, and her placenta had failed. She was no longer able to provide her unborn baby with the proper nutrients he needed to grow while still in her womb.

They had checked regularly every two weeks, but something had happened this time which resulted in an obstetrical emergency. The baby would have to be delivered immediately, three weeks early.

All of a sudden, this pregnancy that had begun so horribly with a devastating weight loss and then got even worse with the realization that the baby was indeed a male who would have the mitochondrial disease was now about to climax very unexpectedly. Estrella and Jerry had only recently come to terms with the pregnancy and had accepted what they would be facing after birth. They had even taken a birthing class and had made peace with the situation. They had begun to embrace the pregnancy and had overcome the initial devastation they felt. Now, everything was dissolving right before their eyes. Their world was crashing.

It was time for Estrella to fight for her baby boy. She was given twenty-four hours to gather her family. All her birthing and bonding plans disbanded, and she had an emergency caesarean section the next day, the day after Mother's Day.

Although he was only three weeks early, it was more like five weeks early in terms of his growth. They didn't know if his lungs would be completely developed since he had stopped growing. What a huge relief it was in the operating room when they heard him cry!

Somehow, Estrella and Jerry had expected to have it all. They had always lived such a charmed life. They were always at the right place at the right time to reap the benefits of a spectacular lifestyle. They had met amazing people and done marvelous things during their marriage and thought life should be no different when they decided to have a baby. Even though she had Sjögren's, Estrella had continued this fun-filled charmed life.

What would have happened had they chosen not to have a baby? Life was good, and things were going along just fine in their marriage, even though Estrella had

Sjögren's. They thought they certainly didn't need a child to enhance their lives because they thought they already had such a wonderfully exciting lifestyle. "We were the last people who needed a baby to improve our marriage," Estrella proclaimed. It was something they had agonized over for years, and after finally deciding to get pregnant, they certainly never envisioned it would end like this.

To willingly decide to take the risk of passing on the mitochondrial disease to a male child was something the Bibbeys struggled with for quite some time. They had finally made the gut-wrenching decision to gather a team of doctors to help them conceive. They assumed that God would provide them with everything they thought they wanted, including a healthy baby girl. They simply thought it would not happen to them, and when it did, it was earth shattering indeed.

The caesarean was especially cruel to Estrella's body because of the Sjögren's, but she survived and was able to go home about a week afterward with a healthy baby they named Anderson. Because he had stopped growing for about the last two weeks of the pregnancy, Anderson was slightly smaller than what would have been a typical size for his gestational age, but for the most part, he appeared healthy.

Jerry's video of Anderson in his initial hours of life in neonatal intensive care is all the memories Estrella has. She was far too sick to bond initially, and he had to be taken away immediately after birth because he was not able to maintain his body temperature on his own. After baby Anderson's body temperature stabilized several hours later, the nurses were able to reunite a very anxious mother with her very precious baby boy. All the overwhelming anticipation of impending disaster they previously felt throughout the pregnancy had suddenly disappeared.

After taking their baby boy home, Estrella watched the video Jerry had made during those first few hours when they were separated as the baby was trying to warm up in the incubator. There is footage of Jerry talking to him and holding his finger. He was explaining on the video that he couldn't announce his name yet because the baby had not had the opportunity to meet his mother. He was cold, he had no name, and he had not been fed. How sad!

Then, suddenly, this precious little baby boy attempted to put his father's finger in his mouth and suck it . . . Oh, how heartbreaking that was when Estrella saw it for the first time, but how miraculous it was that she instantly felt closer to her baby than ever after seeing him lying there so pathetically helpless without her to comfort him. Never again would he ever feel that way, she vowed. Anderson had quite simply stolen their hearts and gave new meaning to their lives. He had filled a void in their hearts they never knew was empty.

God had indeed blessed them with exactly what they needed, a wonderful, intelligent baby boy with a disease that may truly have a cure in his lifetime. Their research geneticist at Stanford is working around the clock to make a breakthrough with this mitochondrial disease.

The most surprising revelation Estrella encountered after birth was that she had difficulty producing breast milk. Because Sjögren's interferes with moisture producing glands, Estrella continues to wonder even until this day if her inability to produce enough milk was due to Sjögren's.

Historically, most women are diagnosed after their childbearing years, so there really wasn't any research at the time concerning the matter. She struggled nearly nine months and wished someone had given her permission to stop trying to breastfeed. But because there was no research to validate this, Estrella was guilt-ridden and felt pressured to try to breastfeed anyway, although she never produced an adequate amount of milk.

Another difficult issue Estrella had to face as a young mother of a young child was how to deal with the chronic pain issues caused by Sjögren's. Most children don't understand when their parents are ill. Although Anderson is now a very active, four-year-old preschooler, he has learned that there are days when his mother is ill or in too much pain to play with him. He has learned to say, "Mommy's not well today," or "Mommy's hurting more today."

He has also learned to be a very independent little boy and tries to help as much as he can. Estrella still feels guilty that Anderson has "a disabled mother," even though he has adapted quite nicely and understands there will be good days and bad days. It doesn't stop her feelings of guilt, even though Estrella clearly understands there is nothing she can do about it. Jerry is the fun parent who plays on the floor with Anderson and engages in very physical activities. Some days, Estrella can't even read him a bedtime story because it hurts too badly to simply turn the pages of a book.

Dealing with the daily struggles of the chronic nature of this disease presents unique challenges for this young mother, but she has met them head-on. Being a mother means she no longer lives for herself. Her life revolves around her son.

Not a day goes by that she doesn't make sacrifices to try to be the best mother that she can for her young child, even when it means being in more pain because she can't take narcotic pain medications and function normally around him. She prioritizes being alert and unimpaired, but that comes at a very painful cost at times.

While the Bibbeys are now well established with an extremely close-knit circle of friends in the Boulder Creek area of the Santa Cruz Mountains outside the San Francisco Bay, that wasn't always the case. They had to reluctantly move to this area when Anderson was merely two months old due to a job change for Jerry. Timing was far from perfect, but it was a necessity that they move at such an inopportune time in Anderson's life.

Chapter 11

Picture Perfect

THEIR WHOLE EXISTENCE was turned upside down when they moved to the Santa Cruz Mountains near California's first state park among ancient redwood trees. It's the last town at the end of winding roads, not an ideal place to raise a young child, although it's quite naturally a very beautiful and serene area. Because Jerry had been laid off from his golf course in the Bay Area, they were forced to relocate for a new job, leaving behind everything they once knew as normal.

Much to Estrella's surprise, there was a tight-knit network of young mothers in the community, which was very well established. Estrella and Anderson attended baby playdates and met a wonderful group of people. Although the idea of moving to this extremely remote area with no one she knew was worrisome for her at first, Estrella now marvels at how "picture perfect" her life has become there.

What an amazing circle of friends they found buried deep within the redwoods of the Santa Cruz Mountains. The area is positively beautiful, and so are their wonderful friends. They have truly become a part of the family.

After being so bitter and angry because they had to move, Estrella has realized once again that when she felt she was in the deepest valley of despair, the Lord showed up when she appeared to have the least amount of faith. It was then that she realized that's when God was actually working the most on her behalf, and the end result was nothing short of miraculous.

Through the fabulous connections she has made in her new home, Estrella founded Team Sjögren's California, a volunteer fundraising organization benefitting the Sjögren's Syndrome Foundation. But even before this time, Estrella was already involved with the Sjögren's Syndrome Foundation. In 2005, she met the staff and volunteered at a national meeting in San Francisco. Two years later, she was tapped to join the National Board of Directors for the foundation, which she has actively served on ever since. Therefore, founding Team Sjögren's California was a culmination of years of service to the foundation.

In the spring of 2010, while attending a Sjögren's National Patient Conference in San Francisco, Estrella was extremely impressed with one of the volunteers recognized at the conference for her fundraising efforts. The young teacher had raised money by hosting bake sales. "My goodness, I could at least do a bake sale or something to help raise money," Estrella thought to herself. "What can I do?"

Estrella returned home inspired to do *something* to help. She really wanted to make a difference and was extremely jubilant to learn there was a very popular 10K race in the Santa Cruz area known as the Wharf to Wharf Race. How could she connect with that race to help raise funds for the Sjögren's Syndrome Foundation?

Armed with the notion that all she had to do was gather a few friends to run in the race, Estrella knew she would have to confess that she had Sjögren's. She had lived there and participated in playdates and all sorts of other community activities without telling anyone of her chronic disease. But, now, in order to enlist a few friends to run with her, she would have to expose what she hoped could remain a private area of her life.

She had never told anyone she was sick because she wanted to connect and make new friends. So she suffered in silence and, at the end of the day, would need Jerry to help her and Anderson out of the car and into the house because she had tried to function in front of her friends as if she wasn't in pain. But now they would need to find out that Estrella had Sjögren's.

She had hoped to gather eight of her closest friends who would agree to join the team with Jerry and herself so that they would have a group of ten in that first Wharf to Wharf Race. Not only would she have to admit to having Sjögren's, but she would also need to ask them to run six miles and help raise money for a disease they never even knew Estrella had. Much to her surprise, she ended up with a team of fourteen at that first race and greatly surpassed her goal of raising $5,000. Her wonderful group of friends helped her to raise $14,000.

Estrella's Team Sjögren's California has just completed its third fundraising season. They met their goal for 2012 by raising $30,000. She had an astonishing forty-seven people run in her honor that year. Even more remarkable is that they have raised over $70,000 total in only three years, enough money to be the equivalent of two Sjögren's research grants. That is absolutely amazing!

Estrella was honored to receive the foundation's highest honor in April 2011 when she was awarded the Volunteer of the Year Award at the National Patient Conference in Washington, DC. It was an amazing experience for her to be recognized with her husband, her son, and her mother all there with her. The foundation has been so instrumental in saving her from losing her identity completely.

Her connection and work with the foundation for more than eight years has given her an outlet to use her visual, creative, and professional marketing and fundraising skills. It has truly given her back so much of her purpose and newfound identity.

Suffice it to say, the charmed life Estrella and Jerry once enjoyed during the ten years that she was a photojournalist pales in comparison to the picture-perfect life they now enjoy with their beloved little boy in their lovely Boulder Creek community. In addition to the annual race, Estrella and Jerry's Team Sjögren's California also hosts many other fundraising and awareness events such as golf tournaments and fine-wine—and chocolate-tasting events.

As Estrella gears up for Team Sjögren's California's fourth year, she hopes her team will again raise $30,000. This will help the team meet their goal of raising $100,000 in four years, all benefitting the Sjögren's Syndrome Foundation. For more information about her volunteer fundraising organization, please visit TeamSjogrensCA.org.

Additionally, Estrella serves the foundation as an Awareness Ambassador for the Defy the Dry ™ campaign. This campaign is an initiative to educate and encourage people living with dryness symptoms to speak with their healthcare providers as soon as the symptoms begin.

Estrella says, "During the last several years, I have poured my creativity and energy that I used to use for photojournalism into helping raise awareness of dryness symptoms and Sjögren's. I am passionate about improving the diagnostic process for other Sjögren's patients and empowering them to move forward with their lives, just as I have."

Moving forward is exactly what Estrella has done. She has embarked upon a new phase of her life this year now that Anderson has started preschool. Instead of simply being sick, Estrella prefers to be busy and sick.

Using the fundraising skills she has learned by working with the Sjögren's Syndrome Foundation along with her visual skills and sense of design and style, Estrella now works for other nonprofit organizations in her community as a marketing consultant and fundraiser. She considers this an area of personal growth in her life.

Estrella very elegantly and profoundly explains her life like this:

> Working as a news photographer was my passion. When I was required to put down my camera because of Sjögren's, I had to learn to connect with others. Today, my work as an advocate for others living with the condition has helped to restore my passion about life.

During her most traumatic times of little to no faith, Estrella knows that God has always come through for her and increased her faith tremendously. She has definitely been on a faith walk of spiritual growth which has resulted in humility and patience.

Wouldn't it be a remarkable discovery and perfect example for other celebrities to take this same faith walk? Hollywood's Walk of Fame immortalizes stars. I, on the other hand, have chosen to highlight a celebrity with much more finesse. This photojournalist is indeed a *picture-perfect* celebrity!

Judy Kang

Chapter 12

Take a Deep Breath and Relax

YOU WILL NOT find in any history book that Judy Pak was born in a Chicago suburb in the 1960s. It just so happens, that was the same year Dr. Martin Luther King Jr. delivered his famous "I Have a Dream" speech in Washington DC, and, a short three months later, John F. Kennedy, the thirty-fifth President of the United States was assassinated while riding in a motorcade through Dallas, Texas.

Judy's parents were Korean-Americans living in the suburbs of a city that became notorious for their race riots during this tumultuous decade. Fortunately, the Pak family was unaffected by the "world" events and were ecstatic to welcome their precious baby girl into their family.

She was perfectly healthy and completely normal, totally untouched by the world around her. Other than her broken ankle in eighth grade resulting from a skateboard accident, Judy's childhood was completely unscathed. She had a bright future with aspirations of becoming an elementary school teacher.

Fast forward a couple of decades to the 1980s because there was nothing out of the ordinary that occurred during her childhood that would cause anyone to believe Judy would not lead anything but a normal life. She did become a teacher briefly in 1985 after graduating from the University of Illinois but soon left that profession to become a flight attendant for the next fourteen years. She even met the man of her dreams while vacationing in Korea in 1987.

Although J.Y. Kang was a Korean Canadian who lived in Canada, he was actually in Korea going to school and teaching English when Judy was there on vacation. The romance began. At the time, Judy's home base as a flight attendant was in Denver, but she relocated to Chicago to be closer to her dream man who was now in law school in Windsor, Ontario. Judy was able to commute from Chicago to Detroit, which was very close to Windsor, so she could go up to see him regularly.

When the courtship did not end in a marriage proposal after a few years, Judy decided it was time for a change of venue. She ran away to Hawaii and enjoyed the exciting single life of a flight attendant traveling all over the world on international flights. Although her job was a wonderful opportunity to experience all the fun and excitement that comes with traveling abroad to places like Japan, Singapore, and the Philippines, Judy would return to her new home in Hawaii all alone, longing for her prince charming who had likely finished law school and become a practicing attorney in Canada.

It wasn't until three years after she ran away that Judy's knight in shining armor came to rescue her. Honestly, there was nothing to rescue her from as she was living a fabulous life. Perhaps it was J.Y. who needed to be rescued from his lonely life without Judy, although I have come to the conclusion that it must have been divine intervention that brought the two of them together a world away from where they first met.

One thing is for certain, when they were married in 1993, thirty years after the world changing events the year of her birth, no one would have ever expected that tumultuous times would return. This time, Judy would not be so lucky as to go unscathed.

She escaped the 1960s totally unaffected by her surroundings, but after travelling on all those international flights during an era when passengers could still smoke on board, Judy would wake up one day and realize her symptoms were much more than just the flu. International flights are extremely long (usually eight to fourteen hours), and being exposed to so much smoke for all those years may have affected her lungs.

This was also during a time when they sprayed pesticides on the planes in an attempt not to bring any diseases or viruses back from another country to New Zealand. That is no longer the practice, but, back then, flight attendants had to stay on board until after they sprayed. What had Judy been inhaling from those potentially dangerous pesticides on all those long flights to New Zealand?

Just when Judy thought everything had worked out like a fairytale, she thought she would be able to finally take a deep breath and relax. She had married the man of her dreams, and they relocated to Denver, Colorado. The air was crisp and clear, and what a perfect place to start a family. Surely, nothing detrimental would result from all those years of inhaling less-than-desirable air pollutants on those airplanes.

About eight years after becoming a flight attendant, Judy experienced the most amazing trip of a lifetime, the birth of her first child, Ethan. Life really couldn't get any better. Normally, that means it's about to get worse, and that's exactly what happened when this new mom woke up one day in 1995 with flulike symptoms.

A trip to the doctor's office and a subsequent chest X-ray confirmed something very unusual was going on with mysterious findings on the X-ray. This shocking discovery sent her into a whirlwind of emotions. "We see some abnormalities in your chest, on your lungs. You need to see a specialist." Those were not the words Judy expected to hear and are words that she will never forget.

Judy began seeing a pulmonologist, a physician who specializes in treating diseases of the lungs and respiratory tract. A year after the joyous birth of her first child, Judy had to face an uncertain surgical procedure. She thought to herself, "This doctor actually wants to go inside me and take a piece of my lungs. Why?"

She had no symptoms at the time, but he wanted to cut her open because of all the abnormal findings. She was scared not to consent to the biopsy, but also very reluctant to agree. Afraid of having something dreadful and undiagnosed, she realized it was in her best interest to proceed. Unfortunately, nothing specific was discovered by doing the biopsy either.

"We think you have some kind of lung illness. We can't pinpoint it. We're not sure." What? That was simply more nonsense that Judy certainly never expected to hear, words that didn't mean a thing because they offered no answers.

For the next three years, she didn't get any better, but, fortunately, she didn't get any worse either. She went for a checkup every few months, and they would do different breathing tests to no avail. Nothing changed. Steroids didn't help.

She was eventually referred to National Jewish Medical Center, the number one respiratory hospital in the nation, which just happened to be in Denver, a few short miles from her home. There, she met who she felt was the best doctor in the world, chief of the Interstitial Lung Disease Program, Dr. Kevin Brown, the man who would eventually deliver some startling news. But, first, Judy had some other family business to take care of.

Even though she was suffering from some form of an unidentified lung illness, Judy had a toddler at home. Add to this happy family of three Emily, Judy's daughter who was born a couple of years after Judy first began experiencing respiratory difficulties. What a wonderful time in her life, but also one of great uncertainty.

Being the loving and devoted mother of two very young children, while being uncertain of her own health issues, was quite a frightening time. She was totally drained and didn't know why. The cause of her extreme fatigue would not be revealed for another three years. Judy didn't know what was wrong, but one thing was for certain, her encounter with Dr. Brown was about to change everything.

After a series of diagnostic tests, including a bronchoscopy and another lung biopsy, as well as an extensive medical history and assessment, Dr. Brown started connecting the dots. Judy had previously shared with him how fatigued she was and how her joints hurt so terribly bad. Those were not the typical postpartum symptoms one would expect to find.

There had to be something going on in her body that was attacking her lungs. She was diagnosed with lymphocytic interstitial pneumonia and some type of connective tissue disorder, but that was merely the beginning of her journey.

Dr. Brown referred her to a rheumatologist who did more tests, including a lip biopsy, and all the pieces of the bizarre puzzle were finally in place. The year before the dawn of a new millennium, Judy was diagnosed with Sjögren's syndrome. At long last, she had an answer, but, now, she would never be able to relax and take a deep breath again because she was terrified of having this thing she had never heard of. Although she was relieved to finally know what had been attacking her lungs, she was distressed to learn it was a chronic condition for which there was no known cure.

Judy tried with all she had to keep the faith. She believed she could find a natural cure. As a child, she was raised as a Seventh-day Adventist, a church known for its emphasis on diet and health. She already had a holistic understanding of life. What better beliefs to be equipped with now that she was facing a life-changing illness.

Judy desperately wanted a cure for what ailed her. She tried so hard to make it go away with holistic medicine, acupuncture, cleansers, vitamins, and naturopathy, all to no avail. She was searching for an answer. Surely she would discover a natural cure. Of course, she would find the answer she so desperately sought after.

Her condition continued to deteriorate, but Judy thought things wouldn't get any worse. Nonetheless, the new millennium proved to be even worse than the prior, and the Kang family would soon discover that, in the year 2000, they would face something much worse than the Y2K clicking time bomb. While the rest of the world was in a frenzy to revise their computer operating systems to make them work as the clock counted down to January 1, 2000, Judy worked just as feverishly to find a way to make her Sjögren's symptoms go away.

When the clock struck 12:01, there were no major problems experienced across the planet. Almost everything worked like normal. The banks didn't collapse, there were no major power outages, airplanes still flew, aliens didn't invade the earth, and the world didn't end. Everyone went on with life as usual. Well, not everyone . . . and not as usual . . .

Chapter 13

Y2K Began with a Bug Instead of a Bang

MANY EXPECTED TOTAL chaos as we rang in 2000, but, actually, it was quite uneventful. Although Judy was learning to live with an incurable autoimmune disease, which had attacked her lungs, she was still a caring and dutiful wife as well as a loving and devoted mother of two young children. Life must go on, and so it did.

Her firstborn, Ethan, was old enough to have already started elementary school by now, and her baby girl would soon turn three. Whew! Those "terrible twos" for which toddlers are infamous were over forever in the Kang household, but something much worse was lurking in the shadows.

What was Emily up to now? She was walking, talking, and already potty-trained. Suddenly, things changed, and Emily stopped walking. They went to the emergency room where the doctor said she was probably just seeking attention. He advised them to give her some Advil and go home, even though she couldn't move her legs.

For a week, they battled with this, making three or four trips back and forth to her regular pediatrician. To make matters worse, Emily started to regress with potty training as well.

Wasn't it already bad enough that Judy's efforts to find a natural remedy for Sjögren's had failed? She was finding it more difficult than ever to try to maintain some sense of normalcy. The fairytale had totally fallen apart, and as shocking as it was to learn that her lungs were being attacked, the next medical calamity to strike this family was almost unbearable and gravely more severe.

Sweet little Emily was not seeking attention as the ill-advised emergency room doctor had explained to her bewildered parents. She had become temporarily paralyzed. Her pediatrician had never seen such in someone as young as Emily. After battling with this new quandary for a week, Emily's pediatrician finally referred them to the Children's Hospital in Denver.

Judy will never forget the elderly Dr. Paul Moe, a seemingly eighty-year-old pediatric neurosurgeon who instantly knew what the younger doctors had failed to diagnose on this very sad Labor Day of the year 2000. They had called him in from home because none of the other doctors could figure out what was causing Emily's paralysis.

With no sugarcoating, and in a very matter-of-fact way, Dr. Moe delivered the dismal news as quickly as he had assessed Judy's precious three-year-old baby girl. "She has Guillain-Barré." This was the beginning of a nightmarish four days. Guillain-Barré is a medical condition that was affecting Emily's nervous system. It could cause muscle weakness, loss of reflexes, and paralysis in her arms, legs, face, and other parts of her frail little body. It could even cause her death.

Emily was admitted to the hospital immediately, and the days that followed were, without a doubt, the worst days of Judy's life as she stayed at the hospital day and night, sleeping scrunched up in a ball in the window seat in Emily's freezing cold room. Undoubtedly, the stress of watching her baby girl suffer needlessly compounded the physical symptoms of Judy's Sjögren's. It was theoretically enough stress to literally kill Judy.

She would not have been the first mother to die from a broken heart. If the paralysis from the Guillain-Barré spread into Emily's little chest, they would be forced to put her on a breathing machine. Who even knew they made machines small enough to accommodate a tiny three-year-old? The Guillain-Barré did spread from her legs to her arms and into her face, but, miraculously, her lungs were spared. There was nothing they could do but wait to see what was going to happen next.

After waiting to exhale for four straight days, Judy and her husband were finally told it was over. It did not spread to Emily's chest, and, over a period of time, they could expect that Emily would return to normal and learn to walk again. She had survived this dreadful ordeal, and they took her home to begin the long road to recovery with extensive rehabilitation. Yes, Emily would rebound over a period of time as if she never had this deplorable disease. Regrettably, the prognosis would not be as joyous for Judy.

Having an autoimmune disease like Sjögren's could have been profoundly exacerbated by this dire situation Judy faced. She had watched her baby girl lie hopelessly motionless in that hospital room with paralysis attacking her body. Meanwhile, Judy's body was also under attack, and, sadly, Judy lost the battle.

Chapter 14

Waiting to Exhale

EMILY SURVIVED AND essentially returned to normal. The only noticeable lasting effect which she still has today is her inability to make a complete smile. Her facial muscles never recovered fully enough to "smile big." How ironic.

Judy also survived, but did not fare as well. Her breathing became so low that she eventually had to go on oxygen a few short months after Emily's horrific ordeal. This became the new normal twenty-four hours a day, seven days a week. Judy was permanently attached to a cord linking her to portable oxygen, which she had to carry with her everywhere.

Seeking answers which were not there prompted Judy to pursue a second opinion. Although National Jewish Medical Center is the best respiratory hospital in the nation, and, undoubtedly, Dr. Brown had become an enduring figure and the best physician Judy felt she ever had, she simply wanted confirmation of this terribly depressing turn of events.

She made the dismal trip to Minnesota to the world-renowned Mayo Clinic only to be seen by another specialist who had trained at National Jewish. Of course, the outcome was the same, and the prognosis was confirmed. Oxygen 24/7—there was nothing else to be done. Judy knew she had to continue the same medical regimen with different medications in an attempt to control the symptoms. There was no cure. Judy accepted it and moved on with her life, she and her oxygen tank in tow.

The years passed, but things only worsened. She tried many different medications, but there was no change. Her lungs continued their deadly downward spiral.

New drugs were approved by the FDA, research was being done, and Judy was the recipient of many futile attempts to slow the attack on her lungs. One drug even caused an allergic reaction which resulted in anaphylactic shock that could have resulted in her death. Eventually, she was faced with the daunting reality that her only solution may be a lung transplant.

Because National Jewish does not perform transplants, Dr. Brown referred Judy to University of Colorado where she was evaluated as a potential lung transplant recipient. Surprisingly, after only two weeks of testing, she was accepted and put on their transplant list. Remarkably, she was number one on the list to receive a transplant. What a whirlwind of emotions.

A few months prior, neither Judy nor her husband knew anything about lung transplants, and, suddenly, she was the first name to be drawn. Obviously, this was merely the beginning of the waiting period. Sometimes, people are on a transplant list for months or years; and, sometimes, they die waiting.

Things moved so smoothly and quickly that Judy had second thoughts. Four days after unexpectedly being put on the list, Judy called the transplant coordinator to express her uneasiness. She didn't feel prepared; she didn't really understand what was happening or what to expect. The coordinator assured her there would be ample time to get all her issues addressed.

They would not force her to do anything or accept a lung until she was totally agreeable and fully understood what she was facing. She could say no if she wasn't ready to accept a lung whenever one became available. Whew! That was reassuring. She could relax.

What happened next was a monumental surprise to everyone. "Boom! Just like that, they called me the very next day," Judy said. "We have a lung for you . . . You have to come right now."

Being totally unprepared for the opportunity of a lifetime, she discussed it with her husband, and it just wasn't the right time. Neither Judy nor J.Y. was ready for any of this. They had not prepared. They didn't have enough time.

What about Ethan and Emily? It was simply too soon; therefore, Judy declined what could have been her only opportunity to receive a donor lung. Judy recalls her conversation with the transplant doctor went something like this:

> Judy: *I don't think I can do it right now.*
> Doctor: *Are you saying no?*
> Judy: *Well, she said it was okay and that I could say no.*
> Doctor: *No, you don't understand. There's a lung right now. You're number one on the list. Didn't they tell you this? You need to come in right now! We have a lung for you.*
> Judy: *Oh, I don't think I can come in. I can't do it.*
> Doctor: *Oh, okay!*

Then there was dead silence. The doctor hung up the phone without uttering another word.

The very next day, the transplant coordinator called Judy and informed her that the transplant surgeon had taken her off the list. She was no longer a candidate for a transplant! Judy was totally dumbfounded at this astonishing turn of events. She was also guilt-ridden because she feared something terrible happened to the lung meant for her, and perhaps they were not able to use it on anyone else due to her delay.

She never found out what happened to that lung but has reconciled in her mind that surely someone else received what she simply was ill-prepared to accept that fateful evening back in 2005.

But life goes on, and so it did with her daily medications and inseparable attachment to the portable oxygen tank. Her dear Dr. Brown eventually told her that she wasn't going to make it though. She would have to get a transplant before her lungs gave out. She had to seriously think about it.

A few years passed, and Judy found herself becoming weary. She returned to University of Colorado, back to the place she told, "No, thank you."

This time, they said, "No, we can't do you now. You have too many complications." It became apparent she would have a much more difficult time because of her autoimmune disease. No one wanted to touch her because she had Sjögren's.

Judy then went to California, but after the evaluation, UCLA also told her no. She considered Duke or Northwestern. She did some research but didn't really know where to turn.

She feared her time may be running out but not so. As destiny would have it, her brother Henry's friend was a kidney transplant doctor at the Cleveland Clinic. "Judy, just call Charlie. He's a transplant doctor. They can do it at Cleveland Clinic. Just call Charlie!" Henry told Judy.

At the time, Judy was trying to figure out where Cleveland Clinic was. She had never considered going there, but she called anyway, and they told her to come on in and get evaluated. They assured her that they did transplants all the time on people with autoimmune diseases, and felt strongly that they would be able to take care of her as well. She made the trip to Ohio, and they did all the necessary evaluations over a period of time.

Judy met a remarkable lung transplant pulmonologist whom she felt saved her life. Dr. Marie Budev, the medical director of the Lung Transplant Team at Cleveland Clinic, was absolutely magnificent in evaluating and caring for Judy; and, eventually, she was accepted for their lung transplant list, but with one exception. She would need to live within five hundred miles from Cleveland, which meant Judy would have to leave her home in Denver to move in with her eighty year old mother who lived in Chicago.

During all her trips back and forth to Cleveland for the medical evaluations, Judy was exposed to many different airborne pathogens. The day after she got back home the final time, she became seriously ill with pneumonia. In the middle of the night, J.Y. loaded her in the car headed to the emergency room, and she suddenly stopped breathing.

They successfully resuscitated her at the hospital, and, as they did so, J.Y. caught a glimpse of something he has never forgotten, the startling sight of his wife's lifeless body lying there just like what one sees on television. It was a full-blown race to save her life, complete with all the action and drama of the breathing tube being shoved down her throat. This definitely qualified as being the worst thing he had ever witnessed in his life. J.Y. thought his wife was going to die.

Five days later, they were able to successfully take Judy off the breathing machine. A few more days passed, and when she was finally strong enough to go home, Judy knew it was time to move to Chicago to wait on a transplant. They wouldn't finalize her name on the list until she relocated. It was time to go, and paralyzing fear gripped her very being.

BETTY COLLIER

Chapter 15

Second Wind

J UDY SAID GOOD-BYE to everything she once knew as her normal daily routine, J.Y., Ethan, and Emily and moved across country to Chicago to live with her mother in February 2010. She was put on the transplant list at Cleveland Clinic in March and grew weaker and weaker as the days passed by. Two months after being put on the list, she got "the phone call," but this time the conversation was vastly different.

> Cleveland Clinic: *Okay, we've got two lungs so you need to be prepared. Get ready and everything.*
> Judy: *Okay.*

That was the end of the conversation. Judy hung up the phone and proceeded to tell her mother it was time to go. They hurriedly packed their bags and caught a ride to the airport where a chartered plane would be waiting to take them to Cleveland. On the way to the airport, the coordinator from Cleveland Clinic called again to check on her. Judy told him everything was going well and that she was almost at the airport.

> Cleveland Clinic: *"Nooo, no, no, no, it's not time yet."*
> Judy: *"Oh, I thought you said go to the airport."*
> Cleveland Clinic: *"No, go home. We're not ready yet. Go home."*

Surprisingly, Judy was somewhat relieved. She went back home and took a shower. An hour or so later, the transplant coordinator called her again and said it was time to come in. She could finally go to the airport, and the plane would meet them there.

Actually, it wasn't a *real* plane, only a very small propeller plane with four seats, which was so loud they couldn't even hear themselves think. Thankfully, it was only about a thirty-to-forty-five-minute flight.

When Judy and her mother arrived in Cleveland, it was storming. They were going to have to land in pouring rain at a small airport, which was on the lake because it was the closest one to the city. They had to fly over the lake, and the landing strip was immediately off the water.

The plane was swaying back and forth; the wings were literally going side to side. Judy and her mother were holding on to each other very tightly with fear in their eyes, but neither could say a word. The expression on Judy's face said it all. "I'm not even going to make it to my transplant. I'm not even going to live to get to my transplant. This is crazy."

The fourteen-year-experienced international flight attendant was absolutely scared to death. After landing the plane, the two pilots turned around and confessed to Judy and her mother. "Yeah, that was bad. That was scary, even for us."

Surely, the rest of the ride to the hospital would be uneventful. After the stormy landing, the hospital's security escort was waiting to whisk her off to the hospital. On the way there, Judy was texting her book club friends.

Yes, just minutes away from arriving at the hospital to undergo a double lung transplant, Judy was texting the group of twelve wonderful women in Denver who had been in a book club together ever since she moved to Colorado. They had been so supportive of her during this entire ordeal. She had her beloved support group praying for her as she headed to Cleveland Clinic in the middle of the night to get her second wind.

Judy remembers arriving at the hospital but not much more after that. She worried because she would be leaving her eighty-year-old mother in the room all alone for several hours where she would sit quietly and await word that her daughter had come through the surgery successfully. Meanwhile, J.Y. was home in Denver making preparations for his mother to fly in from Toronto to take care of the children, and then he could jump on a flight to Cleveland that very same day.

The last thing Judy remembers is being prepped for surgery, and when she woke up almost two weeks later in the intensive care unit, she had two new lungs. Obviously, there were many things that occurred after Judy arrived at the hospital in the wee hours of the morning on May 18 until they allowed her to slowly come off the sedation and awaken a few days after surgery.

There had been complications during surgery with internal bleeding. The surgeons had to leave her chest open for a couple of days, and then she returned to the operating room on her forty-seventh birthday to have her chest closed. What a magnificent birthday gift, a tremendous blessing, a new life with new lungs.

A couple of weeks prior to moving from Denver to Chicago, Judy ingeniously planned ahead by signing up on a website for people or family members with serious illnesses that allows loved ones to communicate with each other, leave messages, well-wishes, and prayers. Judy could update all her family and friends at the same time, which was much more convenient than individual phone calls and emails. I've viewed the website, and it was as if I was reading her personal journal which chronicled her entire experience from the time she was put on the transplant list at Cleveland Clinic.

After surgery, J.Y. updated family and friends using the same website. It was a tremendous gift for Judy because she was able to read everything after she had recovered from surgery.

During the initial days following her transplant, she was kept sedated and was much too weak to comprehend the seriousness of her situation. She didn't realize how much J.Y. had endured those initial two to three weeks following surgery when she was still on the breathing machine and in ICU.

He was there all alone as Judy slowly recovered until her sister Marlene arrived to relieve him. J.Y. was then able to return to Denver to be with Ethan and Emily during this immensely stressful time while Marlene began her two-week shift at the hospital. Marlene arrived just in time to dote over Judy and meet her every need after she transferred from ICU to a regular hospital room.

Judy had a wonderful support system, and there were many family members who came to be with her during the initial recovery period and subsequent rehabilitation prior to leaving Cleveland two months after the transplant.

There were many ups and downs, disappointments and setbacks, but, ultimately, Judy got better. She eventually started breathing on her own, talking, walking, and eating again. They all kept her journal entries updated in order for the rest of her family and friends to watch her progress and continue to leave prayers and well wishes.

One of the most poignant memories Judy recalls is after she was in the rehabilitation unit. She was finally able to be free of the oxygen, which had been her constant companion for the prior nine years.

Just as Judy was encouraged and strengthened after reading the journal entries J.Y. and other family members posted on her behalf on the Caring Bridge website, so was I. Below is an excerpt from one of the initial entries J.Y. made the first day after surgery.

> Hi, everyone. It's just past 11:00 pm in Cleveland, and I just visited Judy for the third time today. According to one of the Drs, she had a good day. Her blood pressure is getting stronger, and it appears the bleeding is under control. When they reduced the sedatives, she became somewhat conscious and was able to follow some basic commands. She is still opened up at the chest, and Dr. Pettersson is considering closing it tomorrow if she continues to stabilize. They have kept it open, which means keeping her sedated and on the breathing machine, just in case they have to go back in. Once it is closed, they can reduce the sedation so she awakens partially for the extubation. Hopefully, the closing procedure occurs tomorrow, on her 47th birthday.
>
> Cleveland Clinic is like nothing I have seen before. It's a city within a city. There are 40,000 people who work here; it is the size of a large state college campus and the customer service of everyone, from surgeons to valet attendants is Nordstromlike. It was ranked the no. 3 hospital in the country by U.S. News and World, and President Obama has said this is how all hospitals should operate.

Dr. Gosta Pettersson is from Sweden, has a thick Nordic accent, and is one of a handful of surgeons in the world who does a certain novel reattachment procedure (BAR) that was done on Judy. He is the head of thoracic surgery, having performed literally hundreds of lung transplants.

I just finished speaking with another thoracic surgeon, Dr. James Yun (fellow Korean brethren) who just saw Judy tonight and said she "had a good day today." Talk about dedicated; he was a part of the surgical team in 140 out of 153 lung transplants last year. His work is his life—talking to people like me at 10:30 p.m. Harvard, Yale, and Stanford for undergrad, med school, and PhD. And I thought my University of Western Ontario degree was academic pedigree! Pertinent to Judy, I'm convinced that she is being cared for by the best and the brightest.

There were many more entries in her journal, seventy-one in all. One of the most remarkable ones came from Judy herself on July 3. This was her first entry after her double lung transplant forty-seven days prior.

Whew! I just finished reading all the journal entries my husband wrote throughout my surgery and "visit" in ICU. I was crying buckets as I realized what he was going thru and how hard that must have been to be alone. I am amazed at what he did, and it just reaffirmed how wonderful he is when I really thought he was in denial of my illness. J.Y., you really amaze me. You are the best hubby in the world. I am sure many of you will dispute that your hub is better, especially Evan, (Oh, Bill, we love you.) but I think I got me a good one.

I also read thru all the MANY guestbook entries, and can I just say . . . I have the best family and friends in the world! I can't believe you all followed along and sent prayer after prayer and all that positive energy. You know I was receiving them all because I came out with flying colors. Well, I had NO idea what I went thru because I was so medicated. But those prayers and karma and positive energy brought me to where I am.

Family and friends, I am so thankful for all you have done by writing in my guestbook and supporting me throughout my "journey" of sorts. You made me feel alive and pushed me to work harder and made me laugh, so I almost busted my lungs! I am so fortunate to have you all in my circle of friends.

Thank you to my sister Marlene, who spent 2 1/2 weeks with me at the most crucial time of all during my recovery. She saw the most progress and helped me so much. A BIG thank you to lovely, MAH-velous Lori Doi! She pushed me and gave me laughs and stories to get me thru my rehab with minimal pain. You wouldn't see any photos if it weren't for her.

Today, I am waiting anxiously for my family and my cousin Helen Oh to arrive, any minute now. Helen will be here all week and family until Tuesday. I get to see Ethan whom I haven't seen since Memorial Day because he is on a traveling baseball team. He actually said he wanted to miss a baseball tournament in Topeka to see me!

Or could it be because he was able to go with the Steinbergs to Las Vegas and play golf for 2 days and ride in a private plane and in a limo and stay in a villa at the Mirage with its own swimming pool and putting green? Who are these people? Stop spoiling him! And thank you, Lori, for the passes so they could fly in business class to ORD and get to CLE for this short visit.

Thanks to everyone for the passes, so my family wouldn't have to spend a small fortune to visit me. A GIANT thank you to my mom for putting up with me for 2 months and teaching me to knit. I don't even know if she can get on this website because she kind of gave up on the computer. Many, many thanks to my mother-in-law, my MIL who is Jong Hee Kang. Many of you know her and know how GREAT a cook she is. I am certain that Emily and Ethan were eating LOTS of yummy Korean food while JY was here with me.

I am slowly getting emails out. Please be patient with me. I am still having the shakes; my hands are not steady. This has taken me a long time to write this. Family and Helen are here. Have to sign off. Glad to be back in the real world.

Feeling the love . . . grateful to everyone, hug yourself and pretend it's me. heehee, Judy xoxo

Judy left Cleveland on July 18, two months after her double lung transplant, ten days after NBA superstar and MVP LeBron James announced he was leaving Cleveland to play for the Miami Heat. I must admit, things have worked out pretty good for Judy and LeBron. They are both celebrities from Cleveland!

After going back home to Denver, things slowly returned to the new-normal life as Judy once new it thirteen years prior to really getting sick. As with most transplant recipients, she felt a certain degree of guilt and depression. In order for her to receive a transplant, someone else lost his or her life. She was thrilled to have two healthy lungs which had not been devastated by Sjögren's, but, quite naturally, it was surreal to reflect back on the journey she traveled to arrive at this point.

Being the strong survivor that she is, Judy has performed volunteer work for both the Donor Alliance and the Sjögren's Syndrome Foundation. She has been the guest speaker for many of their events, sharing her remarkable journey which has encouraged and motivated countless others. Her message is twofold because it includes not only being a Sjögren's patient, but also being a double lung transplant recipient.

Judy's message to others: "Surround yourself with a good support system. Make sure you have a good network of people who understand what you're going through. Maintain a positive attitude. Keep a good outlook on things. Believe that something will work out. Live your life in a positive way and deal with things as they come. Take what life throws at you, and do your best with it. Never give up, and continue living your life." That's exactly what Judy has done, and, in my book, that makes her quite a celebrity indeed!

Lynn Petruzzi

Chapter 16

Just the Right Type

THE INTERNET MOVIE Database (IMDb) is the world's most popular and authoritative source for movie, television, and celebrity content. It even allows users to sort by STARmeter, ranking the most popular people in specific categories. For example, the top ten most popular females born in 1956 according to IMDb include this very impressive list of actresses:

1. Linda Hamilton
2. Carrie Fisher
3. Kim Cattrall
4. Joan Allen
5. Geena Davis
6. Dana Delany
7. Rita Wilson
8. Mimi Rogers
9. Sela Ward
10. Bo Derek

Although most Americans who keep up with current movies and what's happening in Hollywood would likely recognize most, if not all the names on this top ten list, there are so many other women from this same era who have quietly achieved celebrity status because of vastly different contributions to the world. In the 1950s, most little girls dreamed of growing up to become a teacher, a nurse, or a secretary. Many of them have impacted the world in very profound ways, sometimes only one person at a time, one classroom at a time, one patient at a time, or one corporate boss at a time.

As a very apparent Type A personality since her 1956 birth, Lynn chose the nursing profession, never dreaming that she would be forced to give it all up one day. Although she would achieve great professional success in demanding and highly stressful managerial positions, she found herself praying one day to find the strength to give it up. She may never make the top ten on the IMDb STARmeter, but she unexpectedly found her way atop a very prestigious board of directors, using her advanced degree in nursing in ways she had never imagined.

For Lynn and her two younger brothers, growing up in Youngstown, Ohio proved to be rather uneventful. Other than having strep throat on a regular basis and ultimately having her tonsils removed as a child, most of her childhood memories revolve around the Catholic schools she attended her entire life. She even met her future husband at a Catholic high school, and their first date was actually to his senior prom.

Right across the street from the University of Notre Dame, Lynn quietly became engaged to Bob when she was a senior at Saint Mary's College. As a nursing major in one of Saint Mary's six nationally accredited academic programs, Lynn was immersed in their core values of learning, community, faith, spirituality, and justice.

A far cry from Hollywood with all the glitzy glamour of the STARmeter's up and coming movie stars, Lynn was a world away preparing for her bright future in an all-women's Catholic college with a tradition of empowering its students with excellent academic programs and spiritual support.

Little did Lynn know, while attending Saint Mary's with a diverse group of women who shared a common spirit and eagerness to grow, learn, and shape, the world, it would perhaps be those values and life lessons learned on that campus that would prepare her for the unforeseen challenges that lie ahead.

As a young wife and surgical nurse with a very promising future, Lynn quickly advanced into managerial positions. She began having intermittent pulmonary symptoms in her twenties but thought nothing of them. She dismissed the dry cough, congestion, and flulike symptoms.

It was not uncommon during times of high stress while attending graduate school and working ten hour shifts four days a week that she would have sporadic health issues. Most women in similar positions would have been fatigued as well, so that never stopped her.

Routine eye and dental examinations did not signal any cause for alarm. Though she was likely exhibiting the beginning of the hallmark signs of Sjögren's, dry eyes and dry mouth, no one would have ever imagined what would surface about twenty years later.

Her dentist could not explain why she needed the extra dental work. He just fixed her teeth and dismissed her. The eye exam showed corneal vascularization, which they attributed to years of contact use. The optometrist simply changed the size of her contacts, and, again, she was dismissed.

The Type A theory held true for Lynn throughout her twenties and thirties. She was definitely ambitious, extremely organized, always in a hurry, felt accomplished every time she would complete something on her task list, and obsessed over her painstaking time management skills. She was a multitasking overachiever who never looked for an excuse for not feeling well. She simply kept going and attributed most of her symptoms to her highly stressful career.

The only time she took a break was when she gave birth to her only child twenty-four years ago. Although having a newborn to care for is not technically a "break from work," their daughter certainly brought much joy and happiness to Lynn and Bob.

Lynn was very fulfilled as a wife and mother, and although she had found a way to balance her home life with her highly stressful executive nursing position managing million-dollar budgets, she could not continue to ignore her symptoms. She simply didn't feel well, and her thirty-minute power naps after work were no longer doing the trick. She wasn't fabulous at forty. As a matter of fact, she was feeling absolutely lousy by the time she was forty-four but had no inkling as to why.

She began having gastrointestinal symptoms, and the medications for reflux did not help. Her throat was always sore. Her glands were always swollen. Exercise, walking, and step aerobics didn't make her feel any better. And then the female issues happened. She was too young for menopause and too old for doctors to dismiss her as having trivial symptoms, which they ignored. As most Sjögren's patients have discovered, it would take years before a doctor believed she was anything more than simply depressed.

Although a pill for depression was what Bob had hoped for, the answer for his wife would not come that easily. If only she could "take a pill, and everything would be alright in the morning." Her doctors did not take her seriously, and many attributed her sporadic and seemingly meaningless symptoms as signs of a woman nearing middle age.

At age forty-eight, she had a hysterectomy. Albeit the surgery did stop the heavy bleeding, cramping, and bladder spasms, she started having horrendous yeast infections afterward. Because of the chronic infections, she was tested for diabetes and HIV, even though she knew before the tests were taken that they would come back negative.

After thoroughly researching chronic yeast infections and the best way to treat them, Lynn eventually consulted with an infectious disease specialist whom she recalls giving instructions as to the type of antifungals she needed and the massive dosage for which she planned to take them. With or without his permission, she was determined to self-medicate, so he complied with her instructions and wrote the prescription for the megadoses. Unfortunately, Lynn's answers were not in the pill bottles. Answers simply weren't forthcoming for her, so she continued her silent suffering.

Her search for an answer eluded her for many years, and, being the type of person she was, Lynn simply endured. Life was challenging, but she was determined not to give up, even though she had begun to wonder if it really wasn't just in her head. Even her doctor told her, "Well, maybe you're just the unlucky one." That was another way for him to say he had no idea what was wrong and did not think too much of it anyway.

Having a family friend who was a physician proved to be very beneficial for Lynn. The doctor had consulted with Lynn about the horrible yeast infections, which left her burning inside; and after all the testing came back negative, she suggested that perhaps an autoimmune disease was the culprit. It was one of those lightbulb moments, although Lynn had not previously heard of this particular type of disease. She advised Lynn to talk to her internal medicine physician about Sjögren's because she was demonstrating some of the classic symptoms by now.

Before Lynn could even talk to her doctor, she did her online research because she knew she was really sick. After stalking Sjögren's on the internet, she came to a startling realization. "Oh my gosh . . . This is me. This is exactly what is going on with me. I have all these symptoms."

Although her internal medicine doctor had attributed all of her symptoms to depression, menopause, and the after-effects of the hysterectomy, Lynn knew there was a better answer somewhere. Reluctantly, her doctor did all the blood work anyway, mainly because Lynn was dogmatic and demanded that she take her symptoms seriously.

Even after all the blood work came back elevated, Lynn's unsympathetic and uncaring physician still would not acknowledge that there was anything wrong. She refused to refer her to a rheumatologist and simply told Lynn that Sjögren's is nothing more than dry eyes and dry mouth. "Suck on lemon drops, and use eye drops." Needless to say, it was the doctor this time that was dismissed. Lynn knew she had to get out of there.

Chapter 17

Philadelphia, Here I Come!

MEANWHILE, LYNN HAD also been seeing a psychiatrist because she had been repeatedly told that there was nothing wrong with her except that she was depressed. Everyone except the psychiatrist believed she was depressed. He told her that she had a lot of anxiety, which was very normal considering the fact that she had all those physical symptoms going on that she could not get an answer to. He gave her a prescription for Ativan to treat the anxiety and told her to keep looking for an answer because he was convinced she was not depressed.

After dismissing her own doctor for telling her to suck on lemon drops and being told by a psychiatrist that she was not depressed, Lynn knew she had to take control of her own situation. Being a nurse, she knew when her blood work showed an elevated SS-A, eye drops were not the solution.

One of the blood tests that Lynn's primary care physician did was the SS-A, which, at high levels, can be indicative of an autoimmune disease. It is a marker antibody for Sjögren's with seventy percent of patients testing positive.

Lynn headed to the internet again and stumbled upon a Sjögren's Center in Philadelphia, a two-hour drive from her home in Mechanicsburg, Pennsylvania. Dr. Frederick B. Vivino was a rheumatologist at Thomas Jefferson University and later relocated his practice to the University of Pennsylvania Medical Center as director of the Penn Sjögren's Syndrome Center. Lynn knew she had to make an appointment to see him, although that feat would be nearly impossible because of his unbelievably hectic schedule.

As she reflects back, discovering that her daughter Cara knew something was wrong with her, Lynn believes the symptoms were more debilitating than she even realized. Cara had started to keep a journal when she was around eleven or twelve, and when Lynn accidentally discovered it while cleaning her room one day, she was shocked at what she read.

"What's wrong with my mother? I wonder if they will ever find what's wrong with her . . . She's in bed when I leave for school . . . She's still in bed when I come home from school . . . I wonder if she really is psychotic . . ." Cara wrote.

At times, Lynn found herself unable to get out of bed. Her sixth-grade daughter would come into her bedroom and tell her, "Mom, I packed my lunch. I'm going to go ahead and get on the bus." Lynn couldn't even get out of bed and see Cara off to school.

After many years of holding it together at home while Bob traveled regularly on business trips, Lynn knew it was time to make the trip to see Dr. Vivino. She was functioning at a bare minimal by this time, and the overwhelming exhaustion had taken its toll. Bob, still being hopeful an antidepression pill would be the *cure-all* to end all that ailed Lynn, found it a bit difficult to accept the fact that everything afflicting his wife was much more than that.

Perhaps depression could cause some of the symptoms, but for all of her disparate symptoms to be occurring simultaneous was pointing Lynn directly to Philadelphia to see Dr. Vivino.

"I knew the minute I talked to Dr. Vivino that he believed me!" Lynn proclaimed. He went through her medical records meticulously and knew exactly what pieces of information to pull out to put the puzzle together.

Dr. Vivino assured her that it was not depression. It was not menopause. Perhaps it was lupus, fibromyalgia, Sjögren's, or some other type of autoimmune disorder. Whatever was behind all this was about to be revealed. He assured her that he would figure it out.

Incredibly, for the first time in many years, Dr. Vivino had instantly given Lynn such a feeling of relief. Never had she been this relieved in her entire life. Finally, someone understood, and he vowed to help her find the mysterious answers which had eluded her for so long.

She didn't have to spend all night every night looking for answers on the internet anymore. She had a physician who was going to figure out exactly what was going on.

Lynn returned home to Mechanicsburg euphoric. Dr. Vivino had advised her to take it easy, lie low, and wait to see what would result from all the tests. Six weeks later, she was diagnosed with Sjögren's in the year 2000. Immediately, he began treating the symptoms.

Knowing there was no cure, palliative treatment was very comforting at this time. The symptoms began to settle down. She never fully returned to her baseline, but she sure did have a great deal of improvement in her symptoms. She couldn't exercise as rigorously as she had before, and she couldn't make it through the day without a rest period. But she could make it through the day!

Lying in wait was another attack on Lynn's body she would soon be forced to battle. This time, it was her hands, feet, and knees. X-rays confirmed she had some erosion of her bones, which meant she was also suffering from an inflammatory arthritis caused by the Sjögren's. She had progressed to bone-on-bone in one knee already, and her level of pain tolerance perplexed Dr. Vivino.

How could Lynn function at such a high level with bone rubbing against bone? Other patients would have been kicking and screaming for some type of pain relief by now. Lynn simply told him, "Well, I told you my knees were hurting . . ." Dr. Vivino referred her to an orthopedic surgeon to treat this confounding bone degeneration.

"Wow, you're too young for this. You need a total knee replacement, but we're not going to do that yet. We're going to try some other things." Dr. John Frankeney was a perfect match for Lynn. He understood her, and he understood how Sjögren's had totally devastated her body. They tried many other conservative options, but nothing prevented the inevitable.

Dr. Frankeney customized her treatment plan keeping in mind how they typically perform surgery and postoperative treatment may aggravate her Sjögren's. He proceeded with much caution and modified the plan to fit Lynn. Before the age of fifty, Lynn had undergone total knee replacements on both sides roughly two years apart.

Knowing this would be a lifelong battle, Lynn had to find doctors closer to home for ongoing medical care. Although she started out very bleakly with the first set of physicians who did nothing but belittle and degrade her, she was pleasantly surprised to discover a second set of caring and compassionate specialists who took her seriously and continue to work with her to this very day to fight the innumerable ongoing issues as they arise.

After a twenty-six-year career in the nursing profession at the executive management level, Lynn realized the time had come that she could no longer endure the stress and strain on her body. She had gone through so much, but after having both knees replaced and dealing with unending afflictions, she knew it was time to set the bar at a different level.

Chapter 18

From the Operating Room to the Board Room

AFTER DR. VIVINO diagnosed Lynn, he very wisely advised her to join her local Sjögren's support group and the Sjögren's Syndrome Foundation. Being the consummate Type A that she was, Lynn did just that. She became very involved with the support group and participated in many fundraising events and awareness campaigns.

She even did satellite media tours with Dr. Vivino. After the tours were completed, Dr. Vivino asked Lynn, "Why don't you write an article for a nursing magazine?"

"Oh, I've never done that," Lynn replied back.

"Well, just give it a shot" was Dr. Vivino's response back to Lynn.

The very first article Lynn cowrote with Dr. Vivino was "Sjögren's and Implications for Perioperative Practice." It was accepted and published in the official journal of the *Association of Perioperative Registered Nurses.*

Soon the recommendation came for Lynn to be on the Sjögren's Syndrome Foundation Board of Directors, and she graciously accepted. She has served on the board for eight years and just completed her two-year term as chairman of the board in 2012. She had an extension to be president and past president.

As if that wasn't exhausting enough, Lynn also joined the Sjögren's Syndrome Foundation Awareness Ambassador Program, knocking on physicians' doors throughout the state of Pennsylvania, handing out awareness kits. "If I, as board chair, am not willing to be an Awareness Ambassador and step up in other ways, how can I ask anyone else to do so?" Lynn said.

During this very enlightening time in Lynn's life, she also started a support group in the Harrisburg, Pennsylvania area and published a second article in *Today's Health.* She has been interviewed for numerous other articles and wrote a chapter in *Sjögren's Syndrome Foundation Handbook.* The sole reason she even considered writing was because she felt it was information people really needed, and she simply wanted to contribute and do her part to help others.

It was becoming apparent to Lynn that although her health forced her to stop working as a nurse in one particular setting, she found many ways to use it in another. She embraced the task of forming a new national committee, the Nursing and Allied

Healthcare Professional Awareness Committee whose mission is to increase awareness and education among nurses and other allied healthcare professionals.

The committee has made numerous outstanding PowerPoint presentations locally, statewide, and nationally and held health fairs. Lynn introduced the Sips for Sjögren's fundraising event in the Harrisburg area to increase awareness about this little-known but extremely-formidable disease. "It has been highly gratifying helping others learn to live with Sjögren's," Lynn said.

She doesn't really recall when she consciously acknowledged that this is a chronic autoimmune disease that will never go away. Lynn found herself simply praying for the strength to deal with it. She has strived to do what she can to make a difference for others. She wants to live the best life she can and help others do the same.

More important than any position she has held, Lynn believes it is imperative to have a strong support system personally. She has a very understanding extended family and close circle of friends. It may take time for others to realize this truly is a legitimate illness, sometimes, with enormously devastating and exceptionally debilitating effects.

One must have the fortitude and patience to wait for others to come to the realization that Sjögren's patients are not slackers looking for an excuse.

It can be most difficult for the ones closest to you as Lynn's husband realized. Lynn's life changed dramatically because of Sjögren's, as did Bob's. What Lynn wants to encourage other families to recognize is that changes are necessary, but life doesn't end because of the diagnosis. You simply have to learn how to make adjustments and appreciate each day.

"You can't expect everyone else's life to revolve around yours," Lynn said. After thirty-two years of marriage, obviously Lynn and Bob have figured out how to make it work. "This is a lifetime commitment," she said.

Lynn thinks things happen for a reason. You must learn to make the best of a situation and look forward to what lies ahead. She strongly believes that you must adjust your mindset to what is a good state of health and accept whatever circumstance you must face.

She encourages others to find a doctor who will take them seriously. Joining a support group is a necessity so that you won't feel that you are all alone. It will open up a whole new world of understanding if you are connected to others who can relate to what you're going through.

Understand that a simple cold or a simple virus may take you two or three times longer to get over, but that's okay. Allow yourself to be sick when you are sick, and understand that is merely indicative of the disease process itself. There are times when you just have to accept the chronic nature of the disease and deal with it knowing there will be a better tomorrow.

Understanding how the disease affects you is crucial in learning to live with it. For example, Lynn loves to garden, but she has scaled back from her once obsessive desire to plant annuals. Instead, she has more perennials which last much longer.

Accept help from others when they offer. You may be surprised how helpful the neighborhood children are if they are given the opportunity to lend a helping hand. You'll learn to appreciate things much differently.

Another example Lynn offers others is to willfully make lifestyle changes that are beneficial for you as well as those who love you. Lynn and Bob had previously golfed together. Acknowledging that her lack of stamina and joint difficulties did not allow her to continue golfing, she cheerfully wishes her husband a good day as he leaves for a golf game with others.

While he's golfing, Lynn is home resting. After he returns, Lynn is able to enjoy the rest of their Saturday evening together with dinner and a movie or out with friends. She has accepted the fact that it really doesn't matter if she felt like cleaning the house or not.

Lynn's final piece of advice is to keep an open mind. Consider alternative methods and holistic medicine. You never know when you may run across someone who can help. It happened to Lynn as she was recovering, not from a Sjögren's flare-up, but from a hurricane.

As this book was being written, the aftermath of a hurricane was drenching Lynn's hometown with heavy rain and flooding. There was quite a bit of damage to her home, and as Lynn was leaving the house one day for a doctor's appointment, one of the contractors noticed that she appeared to be seven months pregnant.

Knowing that was not the case, the unassuming contractor recognized that Lynn was suffering from gastroparesis. The condition causes partial paralysis of the stomach, which results in food remaining in the stomach for a longer period of time than normal. Some people mistakenly view the resulting distended abdomen as a sign of pregnancy. However, this atypical contractor, who should have been concentrating on making the home repairs, asked Lynn if she had gastroparesis just by looking at her stomach.

Shocked at such a question, Lynn asked him, "How would you know that?" Even more shocking was his response. "Because my wife has it." A flat out discussion ensued after this startling revelation.

Of all the unlikely ways this masters-prepared nurse, highly knowledgeable of Sjögren's syndrome who had just served as the foundation's chairman of the board, Lynn eagerly took the referral information and scheduled an appointment to see the registered nurse practicing holistic medicine who had greatly impacted the contractor's wife's well-being.

Lynn is simply living life to the fullest. She absolutely loved her life as a nurse. She has learned to accept her life as a Sjögren's patient. Lynn knows there is someone in control of her life, and she hopes for a better future.

She has definitely set the bar at a different level for feeling well and living well. She knows when not to accept the advice of an ignorant physician who told her to suck on lemon drops and when to accept the advice of an open-minded contractor. She didn't make IMDb's top ten female actresses born in 1956. But she certainly made my celebrity panel list!

Paula Beth Sosin

Chapter 19

It All Started at Ben & Jerry's

THERE'S SOMETHING VERY special about Ben & Jerry's Ice Cream Free-Cone Day. Often, the queue lines snake around the block as hungry and eager fans clamor for a taste of one of Ben & Jerry's iconic flavors, like Cherry Garcia and Chocolate Chip Cookie Dough, or sample a brand new offering, such as one of the four Greek Frozen Yogurts. More people are enjoying Free-Cone Day in more faraway places as the Scoop Shops number approximately eight hundred around the globe from Europe to Asia and back to North America.

Fans are more than willing to be a part of something fun and seem to enjoy their desserts from the company with a bottom line that is measured more than just by financial profit. Ben & Jerry's ice cream lovers come and enjoy the scene, the energy, and the good vibe.

Every year since 1979, Ben & Jerry's fans have asked the same question: "Why? Why do you give away free ice cream on your anniversary?" The answer hasn't changed since that fateful day, to celebrate the ice cream maker's first year of business.

Cofounders Ben Cohen and Jerry Greenfield created Free-Cone Day as a "thank you" to the community that supported their business. While a lot has changed over the years, the company has never failed to hold the annual giveaway to throw open the doors and continue the tradition.

Husband and wife, Marc and Bonnie Sosin, owners of a local Ben & Jerry's store in Rockville, Maryland eagerly support Free-Cone Day every year. Little did they know, their bouncing baby girl who was born in 1989 would later become the face of the worthy charitable organization for which thousands of dollars get allocated through the Ben & Jerry's Free-Cone Day donations or that they would one day begin hosting another annual event at their ice cream shop, *Smoothies for Paula*.

Although Bonnie was a nutritionist by profession with her own weight-loss business, she didn't allow the nutritional counseling and behavioral modification that she offered her clients interfere with having a good time at the ice cream shop. I'm not sure, but I think ice cream can be considered healthy, can't it?

After their first child Paula was born, things couldn't be any better. Paula was a very healthy child, and they lived a health-conscious suburban lifestyle that promoted nutritional eating and exercise.

As a young girl, Paula was always very health-conscious and an extremely hard worker. She excelled in school with straight As and always made the honor roll. It wasn't easy, and she had to study all the time, which didn't allow for a lot of social activities with friends.

Additionally, she sang and played the flute while growing up and experimented with different types of artistic endeavors. Her creative mind came in very handy with school projects because she always had conceptual ideas that no one else thought of. Of course, her teachers adored her and thought she was very sweet.

She was guilty of self-inflicted high standards which no one held her accountable to except herself. That was simply what she expected of herself, nothing but the best, and she always strived to do just that, her very best.

Her family was very close and did a lot of things together. Her younger brother by three years, Yale, was very much involved in acting. She remembers attending many of his shows in which he played a lead role. With two small children at home, Paula's mother gave up her profession as a nutritionist to become a homemaker and focus on her husband's business by staying involved in any way that she could. This picturesque suburbanite family was living the American dream. What, if anything, could ever possibly happen to change that?

While being very involved in her synagogue growing up, Paula understood her Jewish background and appreciated it very much. Just as expected, she embraced her rite of passage by studying and learning the scripts of the Torah for her Bat-Mitzvah at age thirteen. Thus, she could properly welcome the new responsibilities of becoming a woman according to the Conservative Jewish tradition. She was confirmed a few years later and, soon, became a board member of the United Synagogue Youth organization.

It was the same passion that drove her to perfection in every other area of her life that prompted her to be involved in *Social Action and Tikkum Olam* (which literally translates to "repairing the world"). For all of her leadership efforts in that role, she was awarded and recognized by the organization and her synagogue.

Although Paula had Raynaud's syndrome (which decreases blood flow and causes numbness in the hands and feet) ever since she was very young and had occasional bouts of exercise-induced asthma, she remained fairly asymptomatic until her senior year of high school. The asthma, however, was slowly starting to disappear as she grew older. There were times when a peer pointed out to her the color of her hands or asked why her feet looked cherry red when she took off her shoes in gym class, but it wasn't a bother to her.

Following her dream of pursuing a competitive art program, it was during her last semester of high school that something began to go terribly wrong. She had already been accepted into each of the eight colleges she applied for and received scholarships to three, but she had her heart set on the University of Delaware (UD) for its exclusive art program that accepted a mere one hundred freshman each year from across the nation. She could choose any art school in the world, but she had her eye on UD—the one school in which she unfortunately didn't make the scholarship cut.

Not only did it have this amazing art program, but since the college has the status of being a university, its students have the opportunity to get a full-versed and well-rounded education outside of just art alone. This was a critical element for her decision-making process because it would allow her to fulfill her passions both creatively and academically. Once she heard word that she was admitted, she couldn't wait for this exciting new path of her life to begin. However, a horrifying and unexplained event happened just two months before her high school graduation.

She was chosen to be a bridesmaid in the wedding of her cousin Erin and, cousin-to-be, Scott—what an honor that could be! Except, Paula unfortunately couldn't fully embrace the honor when, sure enough, the day arrived, and everything became a blur. Not because it happened so fast, which is how most describe these unbelievably happy times, but because she literally phased in and out during that period of twenty-four hours starting from one of the most important moments of that single day.

The day of the Connecticut wedding arrived and the ceremony went perfect as planned. Paula remembers standing outside of the main dance room, ready for the cue to be welcomed on stage with the rest of the bridesmaids and groomsmen when, all of a sudden, her feet started swaying from underneath her. She randomly began losing her balance and felt too dizzy to take another step. This was the most important moment of the night, other than the wedding vows, which were already exchanged, in which the bride is reintroduced to the rest of the attendees.

There was no way that Paula would allow herself to ruin the moment. Ken, the groomsman who she was paired up with and was thankfully standing beside her, took her hand and wouldn't let her fall. She did her best to gain her composure and continue. And she had no problems for the next half-hour.

The dancing had started to pick up and the toasts had already begun. Then she was tapped on the shoulder for a dance. That single tap from Ken did her in for the night. She fainted, he caught her, and, from then on, Paula remembers very little. Apparently, she was lead to the bathroom trying to hold herself up by the sink, to splash some water on her face.

She went back to where the main reception was held and forced herself to be a witness to as much as she could. But, looking back, Paula realizes now that for the rest of the night and the next couple weeks, she was not herself.

Soon after she got home from Connecticut, Paula was going to try to get some answers. Her primary doctor suggested she go straight to the emergency room.

She was hospitalized under the care of a neurologist for about a week when they ran numerous tests including cat scans, EEGs, MRIs, a spinal tap, and even a psychiatric evaluation—if you thought of it, she probably had it. In the end, they just presumed that she had postviral encephalitis. Years later, she would seriously question this diagnosis.

Anyway, she went back to school gradually (still taken aback by the recurrences) and in a somewhat fragile state, but she had a few more weeks of high school to complete. She caught up on her classes and graduated with high honors.

Before the summer's end, she scheduled to have her wisdom teeth pulled since she knew she was going to need some recovery time. Paula was fervent on getting that out of the way. She lost a little weight from being on that all-liquid and soft-food diet for the week but had to gather some strength and get herself together for college.

She put all stresses aside and was ready to venture on the two-hour move up north to begin her first semester in college. But seeing the weight come off, after adjusting her normal eating habits soon after, she lost a total of twenty pounds over the course of the next couple months while away at this new school. She wondered what was happening because she noticed that the more she consumed, the more she would lose.

Most of her friends were gaining the "freshman fifteen" (pounds) or "freshman fifty" (as it used to be) because of the sudden change of eating habits after going to college, and here she was going in the opposite direction! She was not overweight to begin with so losing that much weight was catastrophic. No one knew what was going on, including her doctors.

Paula started having dizzy spells and would become very cold although the surrounding temperature was normal. It was during this time that she remembers suddenly ending up in the hospital with dehydration, extremely low heart rate, and no real cause of why times like these were recurring. While juggling a full load of college classes, she occasionally had to take time off to visit doctors and the hospital in Maryland to hopefully sort out what was happening. She went from doctor to doctor in search of someone who could help.

As part of a tight-knit freshman class of one hundred following their dreams in the competitive art program, Paula found herself having more and more difficulty with the severe coldness as well as the numbness and tingling in her hands. At one point, the coldness was so bad that she had ten blankets covering her and still wasn't warm. When she checked her temperature, it was a startling ninety-five degrees. She simply suffered in silence.

Over the next few months, Paula discovered her resumé was growing, but, instead of adding exciting extracurriculars to her fine art accomplishments, she added more and more medical conditions and unknowns, which threatened her very existence and possibly her ability to stay in the program.

The doctors back in Maryland could not understand these vague symptoms and why she had suddenly gotten so sick. After a couple of months, she was diagnosed with Hashimoto's thyroiditis. Her thyroid was hyperactive, which meant she could possibly suffer from a wide variety of symptoms because every function of her body could "speed up." Most people are diagnosed with the disease with an underactive thyroid and at a much older age. This made treating Paula a challenge, as she was definitely a unique case.

Nervousness, irritability, increased perspiration, heart racing, hand tremors, anxiety, change in sleep patterns, thinning of the skin, fine brittle hair, loss of hair, constipation, achiness, fatigue, and muscular weakness could all result. It certainly did explain her sudden and dramatic weight loss and all the new symptoms she was experiencing. What a frightening thing to hear for an eighteen-year-old girl who had just recently committed to a rigorous art program at University of Delaware.

Paula pondered, "I'm an art student and found it very frustrating when I physically could not do what I am passionate about." Now, facing an incurable autoimmune disease, Paula was determined not to let this stop her.

She returned back to her normal schedule of classes and finished off her freshman and sophomore year with many uncertainties. This self-described perfectionist was no longer in control of her physical body and was learning that obtaining an art degree would be much more difficult than she ever imagined.

Chapter 20

Are You Dry?

P AULA WAS GETTING very afraid. She never knew when her symptoms would flare up. She told no one at school and only confided in her parents and doctors. There were times she was so ill, she simply could not get out of bed. Her bones and joints ached terribly, and depending on her hands to produce the art was nearly impossible.

Should she tell her professors? Did they need to know the specifics of her diagnosis? Would they label her?

Paula was seeing a rheumatologist and an endocrinologist at Johns Hopkins University. That's where her resumé began to expand even more. In addition to the Raynaud's syndrome and Hashimoto's thyroiditis, her illustrious list grew even more.

- Fibromyalgia
- Peripheral Neuropathy
- Vitamin D Deficiency
- Anemia
- Bradycardia

What else could go wrong?

She was developing a growing list of symptoms, and her doctor list was beginning to grow too, including doctors at Johns Hopkins University Hospital as well as numerous local doctors. Then a friend at her synagogue who was also a doctor suggested she try to get into the National Institute of Health in Maryland. They had different specialty groups and would have to figure out which clinic to put her in.

Paula decided to take up the recommendation to see if she would even qualify to be accepted. On the phone call, the questions began as they tried to determine where she would benefit the most.

"Do you have Hashimoto's?" Paula answered, "Yes."

"Do you have Fibromyalgia?" Paula answered, "Yes."

"Do you have Raynaud's?" Paula answered, "Yes."

And then they randomly asked, "Are you dry?" Paula answered, "I don't think so." She simply thought she was always thirsty because she drank eight or nine bottles of water per day. As Oprah would say, this was the first "aha moment." Once again, this self-motivated overachiever had answered all the questions correctly, and she was admitted to the Sjögren's Clinic at the National Institute of Health.

Paula endured a three-day study at the clinic where they tested her for everything. Most tests came back borderline, so they told her to come back in six months. Being the notable patient that she was at age nineteen, Paula accelerated during the wait period. When she returned to the institute six months later, she had developed an undeniable case of Sjögren's, one of the most unique cases they had ever seen.

Suddenly, she had full blown Sjögren's. She had little-to-no tears and barely any saliva in her mouth. The doctors had never seen a patient develop such radical changes emerge over the short time span that she had been a participant in their patient study, much less in a girl at Paula's age.

What a drastic change in only six months. What a surprise that it would happen to someone this young. After all, Sjögren's is usually found in women in their mid-to-late forties or older.

The dryness was so bad that she could never apply enough lotion, sip enough water, or squeeze enough tubes of eye drops in her eyes. Any or all of her symptoms would come on at any time, often, when she least expected it. The frequent exacerbations proved to be cruel and unusual punishment. Much worse, when her Sjögren's flared, her symptoms of the fibromyalgia and the Hashimoto's would act up alongside this new disease.

At last, her resumé was now complete, or was it? Sjögren's was the most recent condition added, but became by far the most troubling. Her doctors told her that although this was not her first diagnosis, she was considered to have Primary Sjögren's with secondary autoimmune diseases (the Hashimoto's, Raynaud's, etc.).

The doctors developed a specific treatment plan for her to try to reduce the symptoms and prevent complications. This meant adding even more specialists to her list on top of her primary care physician, endocrinologist and rheumatologist.

Because of the classic dry eyes and dry mouth that she recently developed, Paula had to see an ophthalmologist and a dentist much more regularly. Due to the Raynaud's causing a weakened sphincter muscle in her throat, she had difficulty with regurgitation and added a gastroenterologist to her entourage. She also had to see a cardiologist for the bradycardia, as well as a dermatologist and gynecologist for other issues.

This once-very-healthy teenager (and college sophomore) who, prior to her senior year of high school, never had any health issues, was suddenly diagnosed with as many different diseases as there are days of the week, and they keep on coming.

"Where was all of this coming from?" Paula wondered. It simply never ended. Looking back, Paula believes that what happened right before she left for college was probably not the "postviral encephalitis," but the beginning of this lifelong journey with ongoing diagnoses. Perhaps, the episode that occurred just before leaving for college which resulted in a week-long hospitalization was a precursor to the development of the numerous autoimmune disasters stirring in her body.

Meanwhile, back in Rockville, Marc and Bonnie Sosin felt absolutely helpless. They couldn't make their baby girl's pain go away. She was at school all alone facing this very challenging health crisis.

Some mornings, she would wake up totally frustrated because she couldn't even get out of bed. Being an art student and competing with her fellow art students was a source of much stress. Not being able to rely on her body put a huge damper on this amazing gift she had and was hoping to share.

Paula had always excelled in everything she did. Suddenly, doing the physical work with her hands which was essential for the degree she was pursuing was nearly impossible.

"But art is what I love, and I had no desire to give that up," Paula told me. She had no choice but to endure.

She had a goal in mind, she loved art, and she wanted to pursue it. By the end of her freshman year, she submitted a portfolio which was selected as one of the exclusive thirty positions to enter into the Visual Communications program. She wasn't sure that was the direction she wanted to go because it was geared more toward graphic design, advertising, and illustrations. Paula was confident about her talent in fine arts, but the Visual Communications was something entirely new.

There were many times Paula would question the next step. There were times she even wondered if she should pull out of college. What should she do? She couldn't just ignore her health, but she had major decisions to make as she moved from her freshman to sophomore year. Not the typical college freshman by any means, but after all, Paula had never been the typical student anyway.

There were days when the pain was so great that she felt like her body was inside out. She simply wanted to scream! Pain wasn't just on her skin; it was inside, and it hurt so terribly bad.

Paula's doctors advised her to try to exercise regularly even though she was experiencing a great deal of pain and fatigue because of the diseases. Being the compliant patient that she was, and always doing what was expected of her, she tried to exercise as much as she could.

The discovery of yoga during her freshman year of college proved to be quite a breakthrough. She learned that yoga could impact her life on a physical, mental, and spiritual level. She absolutely loved it. Yoga felt like it massaged her on the inside. She was able to get in to where the pain was, like she had never been able to before, and that was better than any medication she had ever taken.

Upon the second semester of Paula's freshman year, the position for the Yoga Club president opened up, and it miraculously was offered to her. So, coming in for sophomore year, she was dubbed the new Yoga Club president, which she held up until her graduation. Eventually, she became a certified Yoga instructor for children ages three to fifteen and hopes to continue making a difference with others through yoga in this life-changing process.

　　　　　BETTY COLLIER

Returning to her overachiever tendencies, Paula didn't stop with yoga. She also discovered Zumba, a strenuous exercise program that involves dance and aerobic elements. She did whatever she could to achieve the best possible health outcome. She would not be defeated by Sjögren's, and, even though one of the classic symptoms is extreme fatigue, she was determined to exercise and stay physically fit. Exercise actually gave her the energy to keep going.

Paula was able to learn the true definition of perseverance and determination. She did extremely well and in spite of everything, she graduated from this competitive art program in four years. She did this with high honors as well: a National Society of Collegiate Scholar, an Omicron Delta Kappa, a Global Citizenship Award Scholar and a Callaway Humanities Scholar. She pushed through every struggle and every setback that came her way.

She had to remain positive in order to finish college. Sjögren's attacked her with a vengeance and never left her alone. It became a part of who she was, so she merely had to learn what to do in order to still partake in the activities that she had enjoyed prior to this devastating news. But, underneath all the pain and suffering, she was the same Paula. Nothing would ever change what made her Paula, not even this disease.

Chapter 21

She's a Graphic Designer, Not a Disease

"I DID NOT want to be labeled as having a disease. I'm not the disease," Paula told me. Having an autoimmune disease (actually more than one) meant she would have to learn to live with this for the rest of her life, but she certainly did not want to be defined by it. She felt like it was tortuous and annoying, and certainly no one should have to deal with it, but she was very scared for people to know.

Once again, back home in Rockville, her parents felt helpless. They wanted to tell people, especially other relatives, but Paula was extremely hesitant for anyone to find out about her medical conditions. Eventually, she allowed her parents to tell others. Then she began receiving phone calls and cards in the mail.

Those calls and notes were very special to receive because she knew that her friends and loved ones truly cared, but it was tough to actually be the person labeled with a terrible disease. Coming to terms with that was definitely new and hard to accept. She was still the same Paula, wasn't she?

She felt horrible at times, and then she realized people had started talking about her behind her back. It was very upsetting to learn that her beloved relatives were asking her parents how she was doing instead of asking Paula herself. In their defense, perhaps they were simply afraid to approach Paula about it, so they felt safer asking her parents, but it bothered Paula a great deal initially.

Reflecting back, Paula realizes that they loved and cared for her greatly, but hearing such devastating news about someone so young with such a promising future, it must have been quite difficult for the rest of the Sosin family to accept.

Imagine how difficult it must have been for Paula. She basically had to remain positive, and as tough as her major in college was, she had to continue no matter what. It was very fulfilling to complete an art project, so, regardless of what health issues she had to face, she stuck with it, and not once did she allow Sjögren's to defeat her.

Four years after being diagnosed with all these autoimmune diseases and other health issues, Paula graduated from the University of Delaware's Visual Communications Program. Her positive attitude kept her going, and she achieved her dream doing what she loved to do.

A few short months after graduation, she landed a job in New York City as Junior Graphic Designer at National CineMedia, the largest cinema advertising company in the world! As they say, if you can make it in New York, you can make it anywhere. I have no doubt this will hold true for Paula.

Achieving her career goal without missing a beat, Paula didn't stop there. It was clear she was not going to let this disease define her. Paula was a graphic designer, but that wasn't good enough. She wanted to help others struggling with the same afflictions she had.

It was horrifying, and it broke her heart to hear of other people living a defeated life, many with far fewer health concerns than she had. Others were suffering more than she; consequently, she wanted to help them overcome their predicaments too.

Paula's advice to anyone diagnosed with Sjögren's or any other medical condition is to not allow the disease to change who you are and that the disease can actually give you the opportunity to view life in a newer and better light. She said, "All it takes is the knowledge of what you are dealing with, plus the effort and desire to endure."

Paula wants people to know that "they are who they are, and they should not let a disease define them. Constantly think about the fact that you have passions and loves and, even if you must change somewhat, there are things you can still do to keep those same desires. This is not the end. Life may be tough and may bring some bad things, but there are also good things out there too."

What better way to help others than to volunteer with the Sjögren's Syndrome Foundation. Her parents have also found a way to help Sjögren's patients by raising awareness for the disease at their Ben & Jerry's store. Remember the corporate Free-Cone Day that all Ben & Jerry's stores participate in annually? The Sosin family doesn't stop there. They allow the foundation to manage a table at their store on Free-Cone Day to collect donations.

Each year, they collect over $1,000 and speak to over one thousand customers. In addition to the free cone of ice cream, customers leave with a much higher awareness of Sjögren's. The Sosins also designate the Sjögren's Syndrome Foundation as their annual charity for which numerous customers at the Rockville store willingly contribute because they know Paula is a Sjögren's patient.

Each year, during the month of May, the Sosins host a "Smoothies for Paula" event. This promotion gives the foundation one dollar from every smoothie sold during that month. In addition to selling a lot of Paula smoothies, they help raise awareness of this disease one customer at a time.

Paula would like to give the four million Sjögren's patients and the additional three million who have not been properly diagnosed a chance to live a healthy life with the best possible care, even if researchers have yet to find a cure. She does anything she can to help prevent others from suffering what she had to endure.

As with most things in her life, Paula always seems to go above and beyond what is expected, and her volunteer efforts are no exception. Along with her lists of various diagnoses and medical specialists that she has to keep up with is her list of volunteer activities at the Sjögren's Syndrome Foundation. Let's take a look at some of her other extracurricular activities:

- Current Sjögren's Syndrome Ambassador
- 2012 Development Service Award recipient
- Annual fundraising with the Sjögren's Syndrome Walkabouts
- Annual updates to her webpage by posting her story at www.firstgiving.com/fundraiser/paulasosin
- Designer of various ads and source materials for special events for the foundation in collaboration with the Ben & Jerry's ice cream franchise to raise funds for research
- Past volunteer work at the foundation's headquarters in Bethesda, Maryland while on summer and winter breaks during college
- Current support group leader for patients in the New York City area geared toward people under the age of forty
- Resource person at the foundation for any young patient who wishes to speak with someone either for advice or just to listen
- Speaks with scientific researchers who are studying Sjögren's in order to come up with better drugs for the disease
- Raised over $26,000 thus far for the Sjögren's Syndrome Foundation

Paula has always been the type of person who wanted to do everything right. Even as a child, she wanted to be the best. She was hard on herself and endured a great deal of self-inflicted stress growing up because she had such high expectations and standards. By changing her focus and viewpoint on life, she has been able to turn this energy around and focus on something with a much healthier attitude.

Being a perfectionist has great consequences sometimes, but Paula has realized, in order to truly be successful, she must not expect perfection. Instead, she has an extremely focused mindset now, acknowledging that true happiness does not depend on being perfect. That's why she volunteers, in order to help others achieve this healthy lifestyle despite being affirmed with a very serious autoimmune disease.

Paula said initially, she didn't put her faith along with this disease but later thought how it could all be a part of it. She had never put it all together until now, so she has learned something new through this book project.

There were certain times when she was first diagnosed that she remembers her parents and grandparents had the rabbi praying for her and for her healing. Her family was definitely praying as well, but she just didn't put it all together back then. She now thinks consciously about the whole thing and understands how her faith can play a vital role in all of this.

Additionally, she has become a happier and more fulfilled person because of her faith and much healthier outlook on life. She is certainly more grateful for her life now, and she understands herself as well as other people better. She's constantly aware of her body and her well-being.

Changes over the past five years have been incredible. She feels she is an entirely different person than she was prior to being diagnosed. Her awareness has definitely changed. She's still Paula, albeit a much improved and entirely different Paula.

Simply put, Paula does not allow this disease to define her. Paula defines herself. By my definition, Paula is unquestionably a celebrity!

Chapter 22

Is There Four Million and One?

INCREDIBLE!
Remarkable!
Extraordinary!
Amazing!
Unbelievable!
Strong!
Fabulous!

These are just a few words that come to mind when I reflect on the celebrity panel fab five. What a tremendous impact they have made in my life. I was still undergoing tests and consulting with a rheumatologist while writing this book. I could so relate to the four million people in America who live with this disease every day. I wanted to be their voices, to share their inspirational stories of learning to live with it.

But would I become one of them? Did I need to become one of them to effectively tell their stories? I didn't know if I had Sjögren's or not, but I did know that I would be much more equipped and prepared to handle it if I did.

After waiting over four months just to get an appointment, the time had finally come. How would this day change the book and my ability to continue sharing their testimonies?

I considered not attending the appointment I had waited for so long to arrive. My fear was that somehow things would change after I got my diagnosis. "Why put myself through all of that?" I repeatedly asked myself. I thought it would be better to go ahead and finish the book first. I had already told the stories of the amazing people I met that have Sjögren's, so it shouldn't matter if I have it or not. The testimonies inside the book are the same, regardless of my personal situation. After all, I'm the author of the book, not the subject.

But then I realized that I am the subject as well. I have a testimony to share, whether I have Sjögren's or not. However, I had already told my story in the first book in this series, and, now, it was time to share the incredible journeys of others.

After my private battle within, I finally understood that I had to keep my appointment because I needed to know. Although there is no cure, the symptoms can be managed to improve my quality of life. Finally knowing what my problem was could be a huge relief. Being justified "on paper" for feeling the way I do because of a medical condition would greatly improve my erratic state of mind.

I had waited what seemed to be an eternity, a very long and uncertain 139 days to finally get an answer; perhaps not an answer, but, at least, a diagnosis. Others had suffered and agonized for years and years of grueling rejection, belittling comments, condemnation, self-pity, and utterly agonizing defeat, searching for an answer that only took less than five months for me to discover. My arduous waiting period was nothing compared to so many others suffering from this same predicament which had obviously beset me. I was indeed beleaguered to the point of exhaustion because I had convinced myself that I was one of them.

So there I sat at Dr. Holt's office, waiting to hear him say those same devastating words that stunned Venus Williams. Was my faith about to be tested? And was I strong enough to embark upon this new journey the Lord was taking me on? Had my sincere desire to be the voice of others battling Sjögren's caused me to imagine I was also afflicted that I had mistakenly and unknowingly superimposed their calamities on myself?

Absolutely not. But what Dr. Holt was about to say was something I was totally unprepared to hear, and I desperately needed the Lord to help me accept the conclusion to the whole matter. And then he entered the room, and I was shocked at what Dr. Holt had to say.

"Mrs. Collier, I'm just not totally convinced you have Sjögren's."

What? I had waited 139 days for an answer, and he didn't give me one. "What kind of specialist is this who can't even make a simple diagnosis?" I thought to myself but never would have dared say aloud.

Okay, wait a minute. Let's hear the whole conversation before jumping to conclusions. What Dr. Holt so compassionately and professionally explained to me was that, even though I presented with many of the classic symptoms of Sjögren's, he just didn't want to jump to conclusions and diagnose me so quickly. I wanted an instant answer, but he wanted a true and accurate picture first.

He had to run blood tests even though they can be inconclusive. He did X-rays of my ailing joints to see if there was another reason for my aches, pain, and swelling. Even after a very lengthy and thorough medical history, he still had questions. Could there be something else causing these same symptoms? He did not want to erroneously diagnose me when there could be logical explanations and, possibly, other forms of medical treatment that would be much more beneficial and treatable.

Finally, I understand why it is so difficult to get diagnosed. There is not one defining test that can be done, not one simple blood test that comes back positive or negative, and not even one infallible method of diagnosing Sjögren's. It is a process that I was merely beginning.

So my wait continued, and I continued writing the book, feeling very uncertain of how this would all unfold. I went back for two more appointments with Dr. Holt over the next seven months before I finally got my answer. (I was also seeing two other doctors at the same time for a sundry of complaints, but I'll get to that in a minute.)

It took 351 days after I heard the word "SHOWgrins" for the first time to finally get my answer from Dr. Holt.

"Mrs. Collier, I don't think you have Sjögren's."

Hallelujah, I don't have Sjögren's!

The invisible illness I thought I had that made me feel so very isolated was supposed to be the answer to everything that ailed me, but it wasn't. Of course, I was very relieved and extremely thankful that I didn't have Sjögren's, but I still didn't have all the answers I needed.

Instead of feeling all alone, as if no one understood why I felt the way I did, I had connected with four million other people who understood the pain and suffering I was enduring. Being told I did not have it disconnected me from that support system, and, once again, I felt all alone and totally misunderstood and undiagnosed.

Even some of the people I thought were very close to me and understand my quandary disappointed me. I had told a few family and friends that I was writing this book and thought I had Sjögren's too. I remember exactly what one of the women said after she asked me if I ever found out if I had it or not.

When I said no, she said, "*I knew you didn't.*" Instantly, I felt invalidated once again. I didn't even bother to ask her what she meant. Perhaps she had prayed about it and thought God had answered her prayers so that I would not have Sjögren's.

What I feared more was that she had simply belittled me much like some misinformed doctors, and my suffering was but trivial in her mind. Even my endearing Dr. Holt didn't know at first, so how could she *know* I didn't have Sjögren's? It took a physician (which she is not) several months to figure it out, and he is a board-certified rheumatologist in a group practice with other specialists who treat many patients with various autoimmune diseases.

I knew that confirmation of Sjögren's opens a world of answers for those who are afflicted. What I did not expect was the same feeling of isolation and self-doubt when Sjögren's is not the answer.

Rest assured, my story doesn't end here. A true romantic at heart, I believe all stories should end happily ever after, and this one is no exception. I am much more aware of my body now, and I have learned ways to reduce many of my symptoms. Some will be with me for the rest of my life, and I am learning to deal with them. I've also seen two other specialists in addition to Dr. Holt for some of the other multiorgan symptoms I was experiencing, and I'm being treated for other conditions.

I was surprised to learn I needed surgery for an unrelated ailment, which would correct some of the overlapping symptoms. Medications would take care of some of my other complaints, and a proper diet and exercise would undoubtedly add to my overall good health.

During this period of self-discovery, I have realized there are things I can do to help myself achieve better health and awareness. Some things are definitely beyond my control, and I will adapt. However, thanks to my celebrity panel, I have learned how to take better care of myself without feeling like I'm a victim of poor health.

I am blessed that I don't have Sjögren's, but I feel even more blessed to have encountered these fabulous women who do. Had Venus Williams never made her diagnosis public, I doubt if I ever would have researched it. I probably never would have related all of my symptoms or sought medical treatment for all the other ailments in my life. I have no doubt this book would have never been written because I would not have known there was a need to write it.

My life would have never been so profoundly impacted by the wisdom, strength, courage, and inspiration these women so willingly gave me. It has been my honor and privilege to share it with you. I trust and earnestly believe that it has done the same for you, regardless of what your individual situations may be.

Yes, I don't have Sjögren's, but my life is far better after meeting these fabulous women who do!

Chapter 23

Absolutely Golden

A S I HAVE discovered over the past year, things are not always as they appear. I posed a question at the beginning of the book. "Who wouldn't want to be like Venus Williams, one of the most admired athletes in the world?" With all her accolades and success both on and off the tennis court, no one would have ever imagined she was suffering from an invisible and potentially debilitating autoimmune disease. When she pulled out of the U.S. Open in 2011 because it was much too painful for her to raise her arm above her shoulder, who would have expected that she would win gold at the Olympics a year later?

Through the streets of London, Venus even carried the Olympic torch on July 23, 2012, which was very befitting as it just so happens that was also the same day as World Sjögren's Day. Below is an excerpt from her Facebook page, which she posted after carrying the torch.

> *Today was an amazing day. I carried the Olympic flame right through Wimbledon! I truly felt the Olympic spirit—participation, giving your best, and bringing people together no matter what their background or differences. This Olympics is very special to me, having battled through an autoimmune disease in the last year. It was my dream come true to qualify for the Olympics. To carry the torch today on World Sjögren's Day was so fitting. My run with the flame today represented triumph for everyone battling an autoimmune disease. I'm planning on enjoying every day at the Olympics—I won't take even one for granted!*

After Venus and Serena won the gold medal in the doubles tennis match at the 2012 Olympics, Venus said, "I had been so determined to get back to the Olympics this year. It was actually hard to explain why, but I knew I had to do it." She went on to say, "It was a tough road too. Fighting my way back up the rankings to qualify for the Olympics was one of the most difficult things I have ever done in my career. But, now, I know why I did it. There is no other feeling on this Earth like winning an Olympic gold medal. And winning one with your sister is even better."

Venus refuses to use her disease as an excuse. Much like Cathy, Estrella, Judy, Lynn, and Paula, the disease does not define the person. What a golden opportunity it is for us to learn from these remarkable women. Although they each face very different challenges caused by a disease that can attack many different systems in their bodies, they all have something in common.

Each woman has resolved to keep going and not let adversity stop them from winning the battle. That does imply that they are like Williams, not only fighting, but also winning. All of these women have given gold-medal performances in their lives by offering a sense of hope, encouragement, and inspiration to others facing challenging situations.

One does not need to be diagnosed with Sjögren's to appreciate the fortitude these women exemplify. Regardless of the life-altering situation one may face, whether it's physical, mental, emotional, or social, a wonderful lesson can be learned by anyone searching for answers to challenging situations.

As Venus said, "It makes me want to get up and fight harder every day." If we could all embrace that same winning attitude, our life-changing situations do not have to change our outlook on life.

I have been inspired by these extraordinary (yet very ordinary) women. They are exemplary testimonies of learning to live a victorious and fulfilled life despite facing unseen and often misunderstood challenges. In my mind, that makes their accomplishments simply golden.

As for me, I'm certainly not like Venus. But, then again, perhaps I am. Because of the awe-inspiring lessons I have learned from Cathy, Estrella, Judy, Lynn, and Paula, I have come to realize I must seize every golden opportunity and continue living inside the testimony.

An Awareness Moment Addendum

F OR MORE INFORMATION about Sjögren's syndrome, please visit the Sjögren's Syndrome Foundation (SSF) website at Sjogrens.org.

I immediately noticed this picture on the SSF website and the list of thirteen symptoms below it. *I had nine of the thirteen which made my self-diagnosis that much more infallible.*

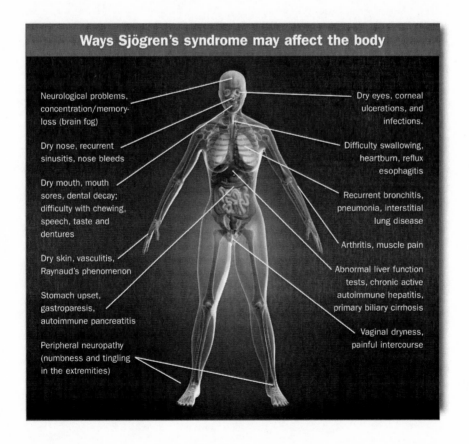

Ways Sjögren's syndrome may affect the body

Neurological problems, concentration/memory-loss (brain fog)

Dry nose, recurrent sinusitis, nose bleeds

Dry mouth, mouth sores, dental decay; difficulty with chewing, speech, taste and dentures

Dry skin, vasculitis, Raynaud's phenomenon

Stomach upset, gastroparesis, autoimmune pancreatitis

Peripheral neuropathy (numbness and tingling in the extremities)

Dry eyes, corneal ulcerations, and infections.

Difficulty swallowing, heartburn, reflux esophagitis

Recurrent bronchitis, pneumonia, interstitial lung disease

Arthritis, muscle pain

Abnormal liver function tests, chronic active autoimmune hepatitis, primary biliary cirrhosis

Vaginal dryness, painful intercourse

I printed the page off the internet and took it with me to my first doctor's appointment so that I could remember to put all the pieces together.

Typically, most patients and doctors would not relate this array of symptoms as belonging to the same condition. That's why increased awareness is enormously crucial in shortening the time to diagnose Sjögren's. It's absolutely imperative to look at all the different systems that can be affected so that patients can be properly diagnosed and treated more quickly.

Symptoms vary from person to person but may include:

- A dry, gritty or burning sensation in the eyes
- Dry mouth
- Difficulty talking, chewing, or swallowing
- A sore or cracked tongue
- Dry or burning throat
- Dry or peeling lips
- A change in taste or smell
- Increased dental decay
- Joint pain
- Vaginal and skin dryness
- Digestive problems
- Dry nose
- Fatigue

You will find a wealth of information such as this on the SSF website, Sjogrens.org. Please start here and visit your doctor immediately if you think you may have Sjögren's.

In Memoriam

IN MEMORY OF Jong Hee Kang, Judy Kang's mother-in-law, who passed away very unexpectedly in October 2012, as I was writing this book. Judy has very fond and loving memories of Mrs. Kang, and as you may recall, she made this journal entry about her mother-in-law while recovering from her double lung transplant: *"Many of you know her and know how GREAT a cook she is. I am certain that Emily and Ethan were eating LOTS of yummy Korean food while J.Y. was here with me."*

Indeed, Mrs. Jong Hee Kang was a beloved member of the family. She was always there to help J.Y. and Judy whenever Judy was sick. Even before the transplant, Mrs. Kang was always available to assist in any way she could.

She dropped everything and flew from her home in Toronto, Canada to Denver, Colorado to take care of her two young grandchildren, Ethan and Emily, so that J.Y. could be with Judy for the first two weeks immediately following her surgery. Mrs. Kang had continued to be there whenever she was needed during the past two years following the transplant as well. She will be missed by many, and her memories will always be loved and cherished.

Thank you, Mrs. Kang, for giving your son J.Y. to Judy. Your gift helped save Judy's life.

For more information about Betty Collier and her
Living Inside The Testimony® book series, please visit
livinginsidethetestimony.com

References

http://abcnews.go.com/Health/w_MindBodyNews/venus-williams-sjogrens-syndrome/story?id=14426884

http://www.youtube.com/watch?v=fsIfOLuCNRM&feature=youtu.be

http://www.sjogrens.org/files/BreakthroughGoal.pdf

http://www.sjogrens.org/files/SSF_Press_Release_Venus_Williams.pdf

Edwards Brothers Malloy
Thorofare, NJ USA
July 11, 2014